# PATIO PIZZERIA

## ARTISAN PIZZA AND
## FLATBREADS ON THE GRILL

KAREN ADLER  JUDITH FERTIG

RUNNING PRESS
PHILADELPHIA · LONDON

Published by Running Press,
A Member of the Perseus Books Group

ISBN 978-0-7624-4966-8
Library of Congress Control Number: 2013943526

E-book ISBN 978-0-7624-5179-1

9  8  7  6  5  4  3  2  1
Digit on the right indicates the number of this printing

Cover design and interior design by Jason Kayser
Edited by Kristen Green Wiewora
Typography: Chronicle, Gin, and Sentinel

Running Press Book Publishers
2300 Chestnut Street
Philadelphia, PA 19103-4371

Visit us on the web!
www.offthemenublog.com

For Grillers and Pizzeria Lovers
Everywhere!

# TABLE OF CONTENTS

# ACKNOWLEDGMENTS

It takes a village, Italian or otherwise, to create a book. We thank Kristen Wiewora and everyone at Running Press for doing such a fabulous job, and we thank our agents Lisa and Sally Ekus!

When it came time to test the recipes, Nordic Ware came to our aid with pizza accessories for the grill. Jim and Joan Cattey of Smoke 'n' Fire let us use their fabulous indoor grills and pizza ovens in the dead of winter.

Thanks to Lisa Mayer of *Hearth & Home* magazine for keeping us up to date with the latest outdoor pizza equipment.

Thanks to the U.S. Potato Board and Eat Write Retreat for showing that grilling pizza—especially one with potatoes in the topping—is easy and fabulous.

And thank you, our readers, for enthusiastically firing up those grills!

# INTRODUCTION

When you go to your neighborhood pizzeria, you expect toasty bruschetta, panini, sandwiches, pizzas, and flatbreads that are bubbly and browned on the edges.

Yet somehow, when you try to make all of that at home in your oven, they're not nearly as good as when the pizzeria bakes them. Why is that?

Pizza ovens generally operate on a higher heat than we can achieve in an indoor oven—temperatures from at least 450° to over 900°F. But what your indoor oven can't do, your outdoor grill can.

Take a grill on a patio and you've got a pizzeria in the making.

In our previous book, *The Gardener and the Grill*, we grew vegetables, fruits, and herbs in our gardens and then sizzled them on the grill—with fresh, colorful, and delicious results.

For *Patio Pizzeria*, we've gone from gardeners and grillers to *pizzaiole*, or pizza women. It's a natural progression because it also fits the way we want to eat—dishes

that are fresh, flavorful, filling, budget-friendly, and on the grill. When we pair bruschetta, panini, flatbreads, or pizzas with salads that complement or contrast with the pizza toppings, we've got great casual meals with a wide appeal that feel virtuous to eat.

Our communal love of pizza began after World War II. When soldiers who had been stationed in Italy came home, they brought with them a love for the traditional Italian pie. But the first American-style pizza that resulted—with thicker crust, lots of cheese, more meat—was not like true Italian pizza you might get in Naples. Mom-and-pop pizzerias opened up across the country, from Boston to Cincinnati, Chicago, and San Francisco. In the 1970s when the dollar was very strong against European currencies and American college students went abroad (like the two of us), they came back with a new/old idea of pizza. Although we were in Rome and Naples at different times, we both remembered how different—and delicious—the thin-crust pizza capricciosa (with its quadrant of toppings—artichoke, ham, mushroom, and black olive—and a baked egg in the middle) was than the thick-crusted pepperoni and mushroom we knew at home in the Midwest.

Likewise, our made-at-home pizza tastes have changed. From the early formula of pat-in the-pan crust from a box, tomato-based pizza sauce, packaged pepperoni, and lots of shredded cheese, we might now enjoy a grill-marked or blistered crust topped with a swirl of artisan pesto, fresh veggies or herbs, dots of goat cheese, and a drizzle of extra-virgin olive oil.

Today, we like pizza because it's full-flavored without being heavy, ethnic without being "weird," and can be customized any way we like it—plain, loaded, vegan, vegetarian, gluten-free, seasonal—the possibilities are many.

Flatbreads, bruschetta, panini, and pizzas on the grill can also have a tie to the garden.

In spring, Pizza Biancoverde (page 210) made with spring greens tastes great with a Grilled Asparagus Salad (page 155). In summer, sun-warmed tomatoes from your garden make Catalan-Style Grilled Bread (page 43) extra good. In the fall, Grilled Polenta Rounds with Sun-Dried Tomatoes (page 59) go well with an Italian Fennel Salad (page 206).

We also like to grill elements of a bruschetta, sandwich, flatbread, or pizza to add flavor to the topping. Try our Big Easy Tenderloin Bruschetta with Parmesan Aïoli and Arugula (page 57), Grilled Chicken Shawarma Pockets with Lemon Tahini (page 119), or Thai Shrimp Pizzettes with Coconut and Chiles (page 159) for that one-two grill punch.

If you like wood-burning oven fare, try a few of these places across the country:

Whole Foods Markets (and their 750°F oven); La Bicyclette in Carmel-by-the-Sea, California; Pizza in Tampa, Florida; Ella's Pizza in Washington, DC; A16 and Flour + Water in San Francisco, California; Pizzaiolo in Oakland, California; Pizzeria Mozza in Newport Beach, California; Al Forno in Providence, Rhode Island; Franny's in Brooklyn, New York; Paulie Gee's in Queens, New York; Ken's Artisan Pizza in Portland, Oregon; or SPIN! Neapolitan Pizza in greater Kansas City and Orange, California.

Now let's get started in your own backyard.

# Talk Like a Pizza Maker

Like any other cooking technique, pizzas and flatbreads have their own lingo.

**BRICK OVEN–STYLE:** Pizza baked at high heat in a pizza oven on the grill.

**CORNICIONE:** The raised, charry blisters on the perimeter crust of a brick oven–style pizza.

**GRILL MARKS:** Browned, caramelized places on the food where it has touched the hot grill grates.

**MEZZALUNA:** A half-moon-shaped pizza cutter.

**NEAPOLITAN-STYLE:** A very thin crust formed by hand, no rolling, and a light hand used with toppings. Bake over 900°F for 60 to 90 seconds.

**NEW YORK–STYLE:** A thin, chewy crust (try the Slow-Rise Pizza Dough, page 35), high-butterfat cheese.

**PIZZA WHEEL:** A rotary pizza cutter.

**ST. LOUIS–STYLE:** Uses a signature cheese, Provel—a blend of Cheddar, Swiss, and provolone.

**TAVERN OR PARTY CUT:** A large pizza cut into smaller squares.

**UPSKIRT:** The underside of a brick oven–style pizza that has a speckled appearance from charry spots.

# Grilling Is a Matter of Degrees

You can do a lot more with your grill than simply sear: You can melt, toast, scorch, blacken, add a kiss of smoke, and grill in a flash. But first, you need a grill.

## GAS OR CHARCOAL GRILL?

People always ask us whether we grill with charcoal or gas, to which we answer yes—we use both. The majority of American households have at least one outdoor grill, which, more often than not, is gas rather than charcoal. As far as we're concerned, to get great flavor and char, charcoal is the way to go—in particular, hardwood lump charcoal, which burns really hot for a terrific sear. But there are pluses to gas grilling as well, not the least of which is you just flip a switch and it's on. You can add wood smoke to a gas grill, too, as we'll show you later on. Just make sure you buy a unit with as high a number of BTUs (British thermal units, which measure the maximum heat output of a burner) as your budget permits for hot surface searing. You'll need at least 40,000 BTUs from the main grill burners (not including any side burners' BTUs) to get good grill marks on your foods.

## LIGHTING THE FIRE

When we tell you to "prepare a medium-hot fire in your grill," this means direct heat, with the flames under the food you're cooking.

When we tell you to "prepare a medium-hot indirect fire in your grill," this means no heat on one side of the grill and heat on the other side. For pizzeria cooking, this allows you to slide the bread or pizza to the no-heat side quickly, if you need to.

## Charcoal Grills

A charcoal fire can be started in any of several safe, ecologically sound ways. We prefer using real hardwood lump charcoal instead of compressed charcoal briquettes. Hardwood lump charcoal gives a better flavor and is an all-natural product without chemical additives. It also burns hotter, which is desirable for pizzeria grilling. Hardwood lump charcoal is labeled as such. It is readily available at most barbecue and grill shops, hardware stores with large grill departments, and some grocery stores. Start your hardwood lump charcoal in a metal charcoal chimney or with an electric fire starter; both are available at hardware, barbecue,

# Utensils for Patio Pizzeria

Several basic tools make grilling easier. Kitchen shops, hardware stores, restaurant supply stores, and barbecue and grill retailers are good sources of the items listed below. Professional utensils are superior in quality and durability and worth the extra money. Long handles are preferable on everything, to keep you a safe distance from the fire.

A stiff wire brush with a scraper makes cleaning the grill easy. Tackle this while the grill is still warm.

One natural-bristle basting brush can be used to apply oil to the grill and a second to baste food during grilling or smoking.

Grate Chef Grill Wipes are small pads saturated with high-temperature cooking oil. You can use them for oiling the grill grates prior to cooking, then turn them over to clean the grill when you're finished cooking. The high-temperature oil doesn't smoke, and it doesn't drip from the pads, which prevents flare-ups.

Perforated grill racks are placed on top of the grill grates to accommodate small or delicate food items, such as chicken wings, fish fillets, shellfish, and vegetables, which might fall through the grates. Always oil the grill rack before using so that the food won't stick.

Cast-iron skillets, oven-proof skillets, pizza pans, and grill griddles are great for grilling flatbreads, filled rolls, and pizzas on the grill.

Grill woks and baskets with perforated holes let in smoky flavor while sitting directly on top of the grill. Stir-grill fish, chicken, or shellfish and vegetables by tossing them with long-handled wooden paddles. Lightly oil all sides of the woks and baskets for easy cleanup.

Heat-resistant oven or grill mitts offer the best hand protection, especially when you need to touch any hot metal, such as skewers, during the grilling process.

Long-handled, spring-loaded tongs are easier to use than the scissors type. They are great for turning shellfish, sliced vegetables, and skewers. Buy two sets of tongs—one for raw meats and the other for cooked meats.

Long-handled offset spatulas with extra-long spatula surfaces are great for turning large pieces of food, fish fillets, long planks of eggplant, zucchini, or yellow squash. Oil well to avoid sticking.

Pizza stones for the grill come in a wide variety of materials and styles. If you're going the terra-cotta route, choose a stone that is thick and meant for use on the grill. A baking stone will crack over higher heat; you can still use it if it cracks, but then you have two pieces to wrangle. You can also use glazed ceramic pizza stones, but make sure you can easily slide a pizza from the pizza peel onto the stone; some have raised handles on the surface that can make aiming your pizza more tricky. Cast-iron pizza rounds and rectangular pizza steels won't crack and are sturdy.

Pizza peels for the grill are usually long-handled paddles made of metal. But if you're used to using a wooden peel for indoor artisan bread, you can still use that outside at the grill.

Pizza oven inserts are the hot new accessory for the grill. Basically, they are dome- or box-shaped enclosures to put on the grill grates of a charcoal or gas grill to trap the high heat in and around the pizza stone.

Keep a spray bottle or pan filled with water handy to douse big flare-ups. (Little flare-ups add that bit of desirable char and you want to be careful not to put out the fire.)

Skewers—wooden or metal—allow smaller items to be threaded loosely together and then placed on the grill to cook. Wooden or bamboo skewers should be soaked for at least 30 minutes before using so that the ends won't char during grilling. Flat wooden or metal skewers are preferred, so that cubed food doesn't spin while turning. Or use double skewers to keep cubed foods in place.

Disposable aluminum pans are perfect for grill-baking thick flatbreads with toppings and to cook fillings for sandwiches and pockets.

We like to have an instant-read thermometer handy by the grill to test the doneness of beef, chicken, lamb, pork, and turkey. For thicker flatbread (page 89) or Panuozzi (pages 220 and 222) you can check the doneness by inserting a thermometer into the middle of the bread: Aim for 190°F.

A charcoal chimney or electric fire starter is key for starting a charcoal fire.

A good-quality chef's knife is essential for preparing vegetables, fruits, herbs, and other foods destined for the grill.

and home improvement stores and most gourmet shops that have grill sections. Start a charcoal grill about 30 minutes before you're ready to grill.

### Lighting the Fire with a Charcoal Chimney

A charcoal grill lets you start a fire by using only a match, newspaper, and charcoal. The chimney is an upright cylindrical metal canister, like a large metal coffee can with a handle. Fill it with fifteen to twenty pieces of hardwood lump charcoal, then place it on a nonflammable surface, such as concrete, gravel, or the grill rack. Lift it up and stuff one or two crumpled sheets of newspaper in the convex-shaped bottom. Light the paper with a match. After 5 minutes, check to make sure that the charcoal has caught fire, or you may need to light another piece of newspaper under the chimney again.

It takes about 15 to 20 minutes for the coals to flame. When the flames subside and the coals are glowing red and just beginning to ash over, it's time to carefully pour the coals onto the fire grates. You can add more charcoal to the fire if you need to, but wait until the new charcoal has begun to ash over before cooking.

### Lighting a Fire with Electricity

An electric fire starter is another easy way to start a fire in a charcoal grill. You'll need an outdoor electrical outlet or extension cord. Place the coil on the fire rack of the grill and stack charcoal on top of it. Plug it in and the fire will start in 10 to 15 minutes. Remove the coil and let the starter cool on a nonflammable surface, out of the reach of children and pets.

### Preparing a Direct Fire

First, make sure the bottom vents of the grill are open because fire needs oxygen. Next, start a fire in a charcoal chimney, using hardwood lump charcoal and newspaper or an electric fire starter. Place more hardwood charcoal in the bottom of the grill. Your fire should be larger than the food you plan to grill: about 2 inches all the way around. When the coals are hot in the charcoal chimney, dump them on top of the charcoal in the bottom of the grill and wait for all the coals to catch fire and ash over. When they've just begun to ash over and turn gray, replace the grill grate. When you put the food on the grate, it will be directly over the coals.

### Preparing an Indirect Fire

Prepare a direct fire first. Once your hot coals are in the bottom of the grill, there are two ways you can create an indirect fire. First, using a long-handled grill spatula, push the coals over to one side of the grill to provide direct heat there. The other side of the grill will now have indirect heat. Second, bank the coals on both sides of the grill. The center of the grill will then be the indirect cooking area. Place the hardwood chunks, chips, or pellets (for wood smoke flavoring) on top of the coals. Replace the grill grate. With an indirect fire, you can grill directly over the hot coals while you smoke over the indirect side. When cooking indirectly, close the grill lid and use the vents on the top and bottom of the grill to adjust the fire temperature. Open vents allow more oxygen in and make the fire hotter, partially closed vents lower the heat, and closed vents extinguish the fire.

## Gas Grills

Lighting the gas grill. Follow the manufacturer's directions for starting your gas grill. The manufacturer's directions will tell you how long your grill takes to reach the temperature you want. Newer grills have inset thermometers that register the temperature inside the grill.

### *Preparing a Direct Fire*

Turn on the burners. Place the food or pizza on the grill grate directly over the hot burner, and that is direct heat. To cook this way, you will ideally leave the grill lid up. When it is raining or snowing, however, closing the lid is preferable. This will essentially turn the hot grill into a hot oven, meaning you'll actually be grill-roasting.

### *Preparing an Indirect Fire*

Your grill must have at least two burners for indirect grilling, preferably side-by-side burners. Fire up the burner on one-half of the grill only. The side of the grill with the burner off is for indirect cooking or for quickly moving a pizza off the heat. To cook this way, as with the Grilled Ciabatta and Grape Clusters with Planked Cheddar and Parmesan (page 48), close the grill lid. If you have three or more burners, you may also set up your grill with the two outer burners on and the center of your grill used for indirect cooking. Adjust the burners to regulate the level of heat.

## GRILL WITH THE LID OPEN OR SHUT?

Traditionally, grilling was done over an open fire or flame. For some recipes in this book, you'll grill with the lid open. Sometimes closing the lid allows you to get more wood smoke flavor in the food, melt the cheese on a pizza or flatbread, grill-roast, or grill-bake.

## GRILLING TEMPERATURE

Most food or pizza is grilled directly over a medium-hot to hot fire, depending on the distance your grill rack sits from the fire and the heat of the fire itself.

In a charcoal grill, the fire is ready when the flames have subsided and the coals are glowing red and just beginning to ash over. This is a hot fire. You can recognize a medium-hot fire when the coals are no longer red but instead are ashen.

For a gas grill, read the manufacturer's directions for the time it takes the grill to reach the desired temperature. Or use a grill thermometer to judge the grill's temperature.

Temperature tip: The moment you open the grill lid you can lose 25° to 50°F of heat. So preheat your grill 50°F hotter than you need it. Then when you open the lid and slide in the pizza or flatbreads, the temperature will drop to where it needs to be. You can readjust your burners or thermostat at this time to so that if you close the lid, it doesn't heat too much.

## Pizza Grilling Temperatures

| On the grill grates or a stone | Grill marks, scorching | Medium-hot fire | 400° to 475°F |
| --- | --- | --- | --- |
| On the grill grates or a stone | Browned, scorched | Hot fire | 500° to 575°F |
| Brick oven–style | Browned with charry spots | Very hot fire | 600° to 700°F |

## ADJUSTING YOUR GRILL'S TEMPERATURE

On a charcoal grill, always begin the fire with the bottom or side vents open. Lower the temperature by partially closing the vents, and raise the temperature by opening the vents or by adding more charcoal to ratchet up the fire. More air means the fire will burn faster and hotter; less air makes for a slower and lower temperature fire.

On a gas grill, adjust the heat by turning the heat control knobs to the desired level. Most heat control knobs are marked "high," "medium," and "low," although some are marked only "high" and "low." On some models, you can control the temperature by turning the temperature dial, just as you would on an oven.

## HOW TO GRILL

Once your grill is at the proper temperature, follow our recipe directions for grilling breads, pizzas, or other foods. Good grill marks are desirable and accomplished by searing and charring before turning the foods with grill tongs or grill spatulas. Avoid turning the food unless the recipe says to do so. The food needs to sit undisturbed for a time to get those lovely grill marks.

## WHEN IS YOUR FOOD DONE ON THE GRILL?

Vegetables, breads, pizzas, flatbreads, and fruits are done when they have good grill or scorch marks and they're tender enough for your liking. Easy.

We recommend that if you're just starting to grill, you use an instant-read meat thermometer to test the doneness of grilled chicken, pork, beef, veal, lamb, and breads. Insert the thermometer in the thickest part of the meat or bread and read the temperature. After a while, you'll be able to tell the doneness of grilled foods by look, smell, and touch. When you touch a beef tenderloin with tongs and it's soft and wiggly, it's too rare. When the tenderloin begins to offer some resistance, it's rare to medium-rare. When it just begins to firm up, it's medium. When it feels solid, it's well done. You can also tell how red meat is cooked by its color. When the internal temperature of red meat is under 140°F, it is red; from 140° to 160°F, the color ranges from red to pink; at 175°F, the meat is brown or gray and very well done.

Fish doneness is best judged by appearance. Fish is done when it begins to flake when tested with a fork in the thickest part. Shellfish is done when it is opaque and somewhat firm to the touch.

# Doneness Chart for Grilling

Personal preferences run the gamut from very rare to very well done. Use this chart as a guideline for your outdoor grilling.

| | |
|---|---|
| **Flatbreads** | Good grill marks and grill-baked to 190°F |
| **Pizzas** | Good grill marks or browned crust, warmed through, topping set |
| **Sandwiches** | Good grill marks or warmed through to your liking |
| **Bruschetta** | Good grill marks |
| **Vegetables** | Good grill marks and done to your liking |
| **Fruits** | Good grill marks and done to your liking |
| **Beef** | 125°F for rare, 140°F for medium, 160°F for well done |
| **Chicken breast** | 160°F |
| **Turkey breast** | 165°F |
| **Fish fillet** | Begins to flake when tested with a fork in the thickest part |
| **Shellfish** | Opaque and somewhat firm to the touch |
| **Lamb** | 125°F for rare, 140°F for medium |
| **Pork** | 140°F for medium, 160°F for well done |

## WOOD GRILLING AND KISS OF SMOKE

To get more wood-smoke flavor from your grill, you simply add hard wood to the fire.

On a charcoal grill, you could add small seasoned branches of hard wood, such as oak, maple, pecan; fruitwoods, such as apple, pear, and peach; or even dried grapevines or the woody stalks of rosemary. You simply add a branch or two, several wood chunks, or a handful of wood chips to the fire after the coals have ashed over. You want to wait to put your food on until you see the first wisp of smoke (so you know the wood is smoldering and you'll get the wood-smoke flavor you want). Then simply place your food on the grill grate, close the lid, and let the food smoke and grill at the same time.

For a gas grill, you want to avoid any debris getting into the gas jets, so you'll want to contain the wood in an aluminum foil packet or in a metal smoker box that you can buy at barbecue shops, gourmet stores, or hardware stores. We find that dry wood chips smolder more quickly, so simply place ⅓ to ½ cup of fine wood chips or wood pellets (found in barbecue shops, gourmet stores, or hardware stores) in an aluminum foil packet or metal smoker box. Poke holes in the foil packet (the smoker box already has perforations). The wood chips or pellets will smolder rather than burn, adding smoky flavor. Place the packet or smoker box close to a fired gas jet, using grill tongs. When you see the first wisp of smoke, simply place your food on the grill grate, close the lid, and let the food smoke and grill at the same time.

## SIMPLE STIR-GRILLING

Stir-grilling foods over a hot fire is a great way to make one-dish meals on the grill that show off your vegetable harvest—and no mess in the kitchen! You can, if you wish, serve stir-grilled vegetables on top of a pizza, with steamed rice, soba noodles, pasta ribbons, or couscous, but they're also terrific on their own.

To stir-grill, you need a grill wok, a metal wok with perforations, along with wooden spoons, paddles, or long-handled spatulas. The perforations in the wok allow for more of the grill flavors to penetrate the food. Grill woks are usually 12 to 15 inches wide. We prefer a bigger wok because more space means potentially more grill flavor and more room for a larger quantity of food. We like to use long-handled wooden paddles or spoons to toss the food in a grill wok. We call this technique "stir-grilling," a similar but healthier alternative to stir-frying. It allows you to get grill flavor into smaller or more delicate foods that might otherwise fall through the grill grates during cooking.

## BRICK OVEN–STYLE GRILLING

To reach temperatures of over 600°F or more, you need a sturdy kettle-style charcoal grill or a gas grill with sufficient BTUs—40,000 or more on the grilling surface.

Place the pizza oven insert (see page 14) and pizza stone on the grill grates. You want the pizza stone and the grill to heat up gradually and simultaneously. Some pizza inserts can be used with the grill lid open, others with the grill lid closed.

For a gas grill, simply crank up the burners on high until you have reached 600° to 700°F degrees.

For a charcoal grill, make a fire with hardwood lump charcoal because it gets hotter faster. Also open the baffles on the grill to feed air to the fire. If you're grilling more than four pizzas, keep a steady supply of hardwood lump charcoal at hand to keep the fire going and the temperature constant.

You might find that once the desired temperature has been reached, you can turn down or turn off the burner right under the pizza stone on a gas grill, but keep the burners on either side on. You'll have to experiment with your grill and your equipment to find the right combination.

Once everything is hot-hot-hot, you simply use a pizza peel to slide in the food to grill in a flash. Because the food has to slide, you don't want olive oil on the peel or on the bottom of the food. Instead, sprinkle the peel with cornmeal or coarsely ground semolina. These coarse granules act like little wheels to help shift the flatbread or pizza off the peel and onto the hot pizza stone. With a quick back-and-forth motion, you slide the pizza onto the stone, the way you would slide a freshly cooked pancake onto someone's plate with a spatula. The cornmeal that ends up on the stone will burn, so you might want to use a very long-handled grill spatula or grill brush to brush off the burned cornmeal every once in a while during grilling.

# Using Pizza Stones, Ceramic, or Cast-Iron Accessories

The reason for using a pizza stone or cast iron is to create a surface in which the temperature is constant, unlike the grill grates, which have cooler and hotter zones. When you put a thick terra-cotta, glazed ceramic, stainless-steel, or cast-iron "stone" over a direct fire, the heats spreads throughout and stays hot longer. Always place the pizza stone on the grill before you heat it; otherwise, if it's placed over the hot fire, it may crack. This creates an ideal surface for grilling flatbreads, rolls, and pizzas without grill marks; the bottom browns nicely at all temperatures, and when you're working at higher heat (Brick oven–style grilling), the bottom or upskirt of the pizza gets speckled with charred spots.

## USING A PIZZA OVEN OR A PIZZA OVEN INSERT

Artisan wood-burning pizza ovens and freestanding gas pizza ovens are readily available for the backyard pizza baker. There are many sizes and shapes to choose from at an array of prices. You'll want to follow the manufacturer's directions when you get ready to fire them up.

When you're deciding on a pizza oven insert, look for several things: How will it fit on your grill with the lid closed? Do you even need to close the lid to use a particular pizza oven? How easily can you slide your pizza from the peel onto the pizza stone inside the pizza oven insert? How easily can you refuel a charcoal fire with the pizza oven insert on the grill grates? Talk to your local barbecue and grill retailer about the best pizza oven insert for the equipment you have.

# Chapter 1

# PIZZA DOUGHS

# Dough How-To

Homemade dough is the first step to a signature pizza or flatbread on the grill. Every ingredient has a role to play. Flour provides body. Yeast, which can be stirred right into the flour, is the rising agent. Honey adds a touch of sweetness; olive oil, a little silkiness. Salt enhances all the flavors, and water makes it all come together.

With these ingredients, a quick stir in a bowl, maybe a little kneading, and time to rise, each dough in this chapter has a particular virtue for the type of grilling you might want to do.

# Directly on the Grill Grates

If you want the easiest dough to mix, form, and then grill, it's the Stir-Together Flatbread Dough (page 32). Moist, tender, and floppy, this dough can simply be patted out to any small to medium shape on a floured surface, brushed with olive oil, and grilled directly on the grill grates over the fire. You can add toppings after grilling. The second way to use this dough is to prepare an indirect fire, with heat on one side and no heat on the other. Then, you can grill one side of the flatbread, turn it over and move it to the indirect side. Top it quickly with your ingredients, close the lid of the grill, and let the flatbread finish grilling for a few minutes.

For a slightly sturdier dough that you can roll or pat into a classic pizza circle, the Classic Pizza Dough (page 33) and its variations work well on a grill with an indirect fire. After mixing and forming, you can brush each pizza round with olive oil and place on a piece of parchment paper. Simply pick up the parchment paper and flip the unadorned pizza circle on the grill grates, quickly peeling off the parchment. Grill the pizza on one side, transfer to the indirect side with grill tongs, top with your desired ingredients, close the lid, and finish grilling. Variations on this dough—the Garlic and Herb Pizza Dough (page 33), Whole Wheat Pizza Dough (page 34), and Herbed Gluten-Free Pizza Dough (page 36), also work well.

# Grill-Baked Focaccia in an Aluminum Pan

To make a thick focaccia with toppings, this method works exceptionally well. Use the Stir-Together Flatbread Dough (page 32) and place the batch of dough in a 12 x 10-inch disposable aluminum pan. Top the dough with your ingredients and place the pan on the indirect side of the grill or on top of two or three bricks that you have set on the grill grates to elevate the focaccia. Grill for 15 to 18 minutes with the lid closed, or until an instant-read thermometer inserted into the middle of the dough registers 190°F. The Basic Grilled Rosemary Focaccia (page 104) and Pepper Jack, Jalapeño, and Roasted Red Pepper–Filled Flatbread (page 106) employ this method.

# On the Pizza Stone or Grill Griddle

When using a pizza stone or grill griddle in a 450°F grill with the lid closed, you'll want a sturdy dough that you can place on the hot stone, brown on one side, turn with grill tongs, top with your favorite ingredients, then finish grilling. The Stir-Together Piada Dough with Red Pepper and Chives (page 37), Classic Pizza Dough (page 33), Slow-Rise Pizza Dough (page 35), Garlic and Herb Pizza Dough (page 33), Whole Wheat Pizza Dough (page 34), and Herbed Gluten-Free Pizza Dough (page 36) all work well with this method.

# Brick Oven–Style

Low-protein Italian flour, labeled on the bag as "doppio zero" or "00," makes a silky-textured pizza dough that can be rolled very thinly. When you're grilling brick oven–style, the heat in your grill is 550° to 700°F. You want a thin crust that goes onto the stone with a deft motion of the pizza peel and is easily removed with the pizza peel when browned and bubbling. The Brick Oven–Style Dough (page 34) works well for pizzas that bake on the pizza stone and require no turning to cook fully. Roll out the dough and put it on a cornmeal-dusted pizza peel, rimmed baking sheet, or flexible cutting board. The cornmeal acts like little ball bearings or wheels to help slide the dough off the peel and onto the stone. You don't want the dough to linger on the cornmeal for longer than 15 minutes because the cornmeal starts to soften and the dough will stick. After you've topped the pizza with your ingredients, you're ready for the big move—sliding the pizza from the peel to the stone. If you're nervous about this, practice the quick forward-and-backward movement with leftover dough, your pizza peel, and your kitchen counter. You'll quickly get the feel of it. When you and your grill are ready, transfer the whole pizza from the peel to the stone. In a few minutes, your pizza will be done.

# Top 5 Pizza Dough-Making Tips

Making pizza dough is an easy process, and these tips will streamline it even further.

1. Measure the flour accurately. Scoop it with one measuring cup and dump it in another to measure, then place the flour in the mixing bowl.

2. Use a Danish Dough Whisk. One of our favorite utensils, this tool with a long wooden handle and a stirring end, which looks like a thick wire mitten, makes short work of mixing any dough. (This is a fun tool and very useful, but an ordinary wooden spoon will work fine.)

3. Keep a stash of instant or bread machine yeast in a freezer bag in your freezer. Cold makes yeast go into "hibernation" and helps keep it fresher longer.

4. Use an instant-read thermometer. If you're unaccustomed to making pizza dough, using an instant-read thermometer to register the temperature of the water ensures you won't get it too hot. Lukewarm is between 86° and 95°F. Check this once, feel the temperature of the water with your finger, and you'll know what lukewarm feels like for the next time.

5. Know your kitchen's room temperature—or keep an eye on the dough. Depending on the season and how warm you keep your kitchen, the room temperature might be more like 65°F in winter (and your dough will rise more slowly) and 80°F in summer (and your dough will rise more quickly).

**A** SIMPLE STIR IN A BOWL, A RISE ON YOUR KITCHEN COUNTER, A QUICK PAT or roll into shape, and you've got flatbreads ready to sizzle on the grill grates. The loose, floppy dough makes irregular shapes rather than perfect pizza rounds, which adds to the rustic appeal. For a vegan dough, substitute agave for the honey.

# STIR-TOGETHER FLATBREAD DOUGH

**MAKES 1 POUND DOUGH FOR 4 INDIVIDUAL FLATBREADS**

2 cups bread flour

1¼ teaspoons salt

2 teaspoons instant or bread machine yeast

1 cup lukewarm water, plus more if needed

1 teaspoon honey

1 tablespoon olive oil

In a medium bowl, stir the flour, salt, and yeast together. Combine the water, honey, and olive oil and stir into the flour mixture until the dough comes together. If the dough is dry, add 1 tablespoon of water at a time until the dough is just moist. Cover the bowl with plastic wrap and let sit at room temperature until doubled in size, about 1 hour. Use immediately, or refrigerate for up to 3 days before baking. Let come to room temperature before using.

WITH JUST A LITTLE BIT MORE FLOUR AND A LITTLE KNEADING, YOU'VE got a sturdier dough that more easily forms the classic pizza circle. For a vegan dough, substitute agave for the honey.

# CLASSIC PIZZA DOUGH

MAKES 4 (6-INCH)
INDIVIDUAL PIZZAS

2½ cups bread flour, plus more for dusting and kneading

1¼ teaspoons salt

2 teaspoons instant or bread machine yeast

1 cup lukewarm water, plus more if needed

1 teaspoon honey

1 tablespoon olive oil

In a medium bowl, stir the flour, salt, and yeast together. Combine the water, honey, and olive oil and stir into the flour mixture until the dough comes together. If the dough is dry, add 1 tablespoon of water at a time until the dough is just moist. Transfer the dough to a floured surface. With the heel of your hand or your knuckles (or both), knead the dough, adding flour as necessary to keep it from sticking, until it is smooth, not sticky, and springs back like a pillow when you make an indentation in the dough with your knuckle, about 4 minutes. Cover the bowl with plastic wrap and let sit at room temperature until doubled in size, about 1 hour. Use immediately, or refrigerate for up to 3 days before baking. Let come to room temperature before using.

VARIATION: *Garlic and Herb Pizza Dough. In a small skillet over medium heat on the stovetop, sauté 2 tablespoons of minced garlic in 2 tablespoons of olive oil until golden. Stir in 2 teaspoons of dried Italian herb seasoning. Let cool, then add the garlic mixture to the dough with the water, honey, and olive oil. Proceed with the recipe as directed.*

**VARIATION:** *Whole Wheat Pizza Dough.* Use 1¼ cups of finely ground whole wheat flour and 1¼ cups of bread flour, and add an extra ½ teaspoon of salt and ½ teaspoon of instant yeast. Let the dough rest for 30 minutes after mixing and before kneading to let the whole wheat flour absorb the liquid. Then proceed with the recipe.

**VARIATION:** *Brick Oven–Style Dough.* The lower-protein "00" flour (available online and at Italian markets) lets you roll or hand toss this dough very thinly. Simply substitute "00" flour for the bread flour and continue with the recipe.

GOOD THINGS COME TO THOSE WHO WAIT THE 24 TO 48 HOURS IT TAKES for this dough to rise—namely, a pizza dough with a slight sourdough tang and great flavor. For a vegan dough, substitute agave for the honey.

# SLOW-RISE PIZZA DOUGH

MAKES 4 (6-INCH)
INDIVIDUAL PIZZAS

2½ cups bread flour

1¼ teaspoons salt

¼ teaspoon instant
or bread machine yeast

1 cup lukewarm water, plus
more if needed

1 teaspoon honey

1 tablespoon olive oil

In a medium bowl, stir the flour, salt, and yeast together. Combine the water, honey, and olive oil and stir into the flour mixture until the dough comes together. If the dough is dry, add 1 tablespoon of water at a time until the dough is just moist. Cover the bowl with plastic wrap and let sit at room temperature until doubled in size, 24 to 48 hours. Use immediately, or refrigerate for up to 3 days before baking. Let come to room temperature before using.

NOW THAT GLUTEN-FREE ALL-PURPOSE FLOUR BLENDS ARE READILY available (we use Bob's Red Mill blend), gluten-free pizza dough is easy to make on the grill. Xanthan gum, a powdered ingredient also available in the gluten-free aisle, takes the place of gluten so the pizza will keep its shape. For a vegan dough, substitute agave for the honey.

# HERBED GLUTEN-FREE PIZZA DOUGH

**MAKES 4 (6-INCH) INDIVIDUAL PIZZAS**

2½ cups gluten-free all-purpose flour blend

2 teaspoons xanthan gum

2 teaspoons dried Italian herb seasoning

1¼ teaspoons salt

2 teaspoons instant or bread machine yeast

1 cup lukewarm water, plus more if needed

1 teaspoon honey

2 tablespoons olive oil

In a large bowl, stir the flour, xanthan gum, herb blend, salt, and yeast together. Combine the water, honey, and olive oil and stir into the flour mixture until the dough comes together. If the dough is dry, add 1 tablespoon of water at a time until the dough is just moist. Cover the bowl with plastic wrap and let rise at room temperature until doubled in size, about 2 hours. Use immediately, or refrigerate for up to 3 days before baking. Let come to room temperature before using.

**P**IADA (ALSO KNOWN AS *PIADINA*) IS SIMILAR TO A FLOUR TORTILLA. BOTH are made without yeast, so they don't rise. The little bit of vinegar in this recipe helps keep the dough tender. Piadine are also great for making fold-over or rolled sandwiches with delicious fillings grilled directly on the grill grates or on a pizza stone.

# STIR-TOGETHER PIADA DOUGH WITH RED PEPPER AND CHIVES

MAKES 4
PIADINE

1½ cups all-purpose flour, plus more for dusting and kneading

1 teaspoon salt

1 teaspoon red pepper flakes

1 tablespoon snipped garlic or onion chives

2 tablespoons extra-virgin olive oil

1 teaspoon tarragon vinegar

½ cup lukewarm water, plus more if needed

Olive oil for brushing the dough

In a medium bowl, stir the flour, salt, red pepper flakes, chives, olive oil, vinegar, and water together with a dough whisk or wooden spoon for 2 to 3 minutes, until the dough starts to come together. Add more water if needed, 1 tablespoon at a time.

Gather the dough together and shape it into a ball in your hands for a minute. Turn out onto a floured surface and knead, adding more flour if necessary, until the dough is soft, smooth, and firm, about 8 minutes. Form the dough into a ball and brush lightly with olive oil. Wrap it in plastic and let rest for about 30 minutes at room temperature.

When ready to grill, divide the dough into 4 portions. On a floured surface, roll them into rounds about 8 inches in diameter. Grill them over a hot fire or on a hot griddle for about 1 minute per side, until speckled with browned spots. Use immediately.

TIP: *Piada dough or grilled piadine can be stored in the refrigerator for a day or two but are best used fresh.*

**VARIATION:** *Sun-Dried Tomato and Rosemary Piada Dough: Substitute 2 tablespoons of finely chopped sun-dried tomatoes and 1½ tablespoons of finely chopped rosemary leaves for the red pepper flakes and chives.*

**VARIATION:** *Fresh Herb Piada Dough: Substitute ¼ cup of chopped fresh herbs, such as basil, parsley, chives, or dill, for the red pepper flakes and chives.*

**VARIATION:** *Basic Piada Dough: Omit the red pepper flakes and chives.*

# Flour Power

There are more flours available today than ever before, some right from the grocery store shelf, others from ethnic markets or online catalogs. Each type of flour subtly changes the "personality" of dough for flatbreads and pizzas.

| Ingredient | What It Does for Pizza |
| --- | --- |
| Italian "00" | Makes a dough you can roll thinly |
| Whole-grain flours | Makes dough with texture, fiber, and nutrients |
| All-purpose flour (bleached and unbleached) | Makes a soft, workable dough |
| Bread flour (bleached and unbleached) | Makes a sturdy, muscular dough |
| Gluten-free all-purpose flour | Makes a gluten-free dough with texture, fiber, and nutrients |

# Chapter 2
## BRUSCHETTA

No patio pizzeria repertoire is complete without a signature grilled bread, one of the easiest and most flavorful appetizers ever. Our friend Judy Witts Francini recommends using the finest ingredients for bruschetta. (Her company, Divina Cucina, provides Italian culinary tours and cooking classes.) She chooses a crusty loaf of Italian country-style bread, preferably day-old, which is firmer. Other breads that we like for bruschetta, including semolina, sourdough, brioche, or challah, sliced and toasted on the grill, can give you and your guests that charry flavor with the ease of a secret ingredient—the local bakery. Ciabatta is fabulous grilled or toasted and is so wonderfully crispy, but beware of the holes in the bread and use with plenty of napkins. Your olive oil should be the best quality, too, more like a finishing oil. We suggest extra-virgin olive oil throughout our book.

As a kind of Mediterranean blank canvas for all kinds of toppings, bruschetta can be toasted on the grill in all kinds of ways, as you'll see in this chapter. Although bread made from wheat is traditional, gluten-free grillers will be happy that prepared polenta, sliced into rounds, brushed with olive oil and grilled, has great flavor, too. You can use prepared polenta available in a tube at the grocery store. You can also make your own polenta, spoon it onto an oiled baking sheet to cool, then use a round biscuit or cookie cutter to cut it into rounds.

The bread or polenta slices should be big enough to manage on the grill grates—you don't want to chase little rounds of baguette all over a hot grill—but not so big that they're difficult to eat.

You can brush the bruschetta with olive oil before grilling or drizzle with good extra-virgin olive oil afterward.

D ID A FEW SIMPLE INGREDIENTS EVER TASTE BETTER THAN THIS? KNOWN as *pa amb tomàquet* (tomato bread) and traditional to Aragon, Valencia, Catalonia, and Majorca, Spanish peasant dish is now a popular tapas offering. An artisan bread with a rough, sturdy crumb will toast on the grill to a raspy goodness that will help "grate" the fresh garlic and tomato. Each person gets a plate with a half-clove of garlic and half of a really ripe tomato to grate onto the grilled bread; salt and olive oil at the table let everyone finish the bread to their liking. If you wish, serve this with cured or grilled sausages, anchovies, olives, or marinated fish.

# CATALAN-STYLE GRILLED BREAD
# WITH FRESH TOMATO AND GARLIC

MAKES 8
BRUSCHETTA

8 slices artisan bread,
such as ciabatta or
country bread

4 plump, fresh garlic cloves,
cut in half

8 medium-size, very
ripe tomatoes, cut in half

Coarse kosher or
sea salt for sprinkling

Extra-virgin olive oil for
drizzling

Prepare a medium-hot fire in your grill.

Toast each slice of bread for 1 to 2 minutes per side, or until it has good grill marks.

Rub a half-clove of garlic over both sides of the bread, and then rub each side with a tomato half, squeezing as much tomato pulp as you can onto the bread. Sprinkle with salt and drizzle with olive oil.

# GRILLED GRAPE, GORGONZOLA, AND WALNUT SALAD

### SERVES 4 TO 6

With only three ingredients, this salad packs big flavor while being easy to grill. Serve over baby greens, if you like.

———— ≈ ————

2 bunches red seedless grapes, rinsed and patted dry

½ cup crumbled Gorgonzola or other blue cheese

1 cup walnut halves, toasted and coarsely chopped

Prepare a medium-hot fire in your grill.

Grill the bunches of grapes directly on the grill grates, turning often, until the grapes are scorched and blistered, about 4 minutes total.

Let the grapes cool slightly, then pick off the individual grapes and place in a large bowl. Toss with the Gorgonzola and walnuts and serve.

**P**EAR-SHAPED SCAMORZA, A SLIGHTLY AGED AND SMOKED MOZZARELLA, makes a fonduta when you grate it, combine it with a few other ingredients, and let it melt on the indirect side of the grill. Serve it with grilled Italian bread and yellow apple slices for a make-it-yourself open-face grilled cheese bite. The sugars in Golden Delicious apple slices make it a natural for the grill.

# BRUSCHETTA SCAMORZA WITH GRILLED APPLE

SERVES 4 TO 6

### For the fonduta:

12 ounces scamorza, grated

1 garlic clove, minced

½ cup finely chopped oil-cured pitted black olives

1 tablespoon fresh chopped marjoram or a mixture of fresh chopped basil and oregano

2 tablespoons olive oil

### For the bruschetta:

1 loaf Italian country bread

Extra-virgin olive oil for brushing

2 Golden Delicious apples, cored and cut into ½-inch slices

Prepare an indirect medium-hot fire in your grill, with heat on one side and no heat on the other.

For the fonduta, combine the scamorza, garlic, olives, and herbs in a disposable aluminum pan. Drizzle with the olive oil and cover loosely with aluminum foil. Place the pan on the indirect side and let the scamorza melt for 10 to 15 minutes.

Brush each bread slice with olive oil. Grill the bread for 1 to 2 minutes per side, or until they have good grill marks. Grill the apple slices for 2 to 3 minutes per side, or until they have good grill marks. To serve, transfer the warm fonduta to a shallow bowl or platter. Let everyone spread the fonduta on each grilled bread slice, accompanied by a bite of grilled apple.

**W**ITH A LITTLE TIME SPENT PREPARING THE AÏOLI AND THE RELISH ahead of time, you can dazzle family and friends with a few quick turns of bread slices and shrimp on the grill. If the slices of country bread are big, grill them first, then cut them in half.

# GRILLED COUNTRY BREAD WITH SHRIMP, PORTUGUESE AÏOLI, AND GREEN OLIVE RELISH

SERVES 6 TO 8

### For the Portuguese aïoli:

1 cup mayonnaise

2 teaspoons minced garlic

Juice and zest of
1 orange

1 teaspoon smoked
paprika

### For the green olive relish:

1 cup pimiento-stuffed
olives, roughly chopped

½ cup chopped
flat-leaf parsley

1 tablespoon capers, drained

1 pound peeled and
deveined large shrimp
(31–35 count)

2 tablespoons extra-virgin
olive oil

Salt and freshly ground
black pepper

### For the bruschetta:

1 large loaf country bread,
sliced

Salt and freshly ground
black pepper

For the Portuguese aïoli, whisk the mayonnaise, garlic, orange zest, orange juice, and smoked paprika together in a bowl until smooth. Adjust the seasonings to your taste. Cover and refrigerate until ready to serve.

For the green olive relish, stir the olives, parsley, and capers together in a bowl. Set aside.

Prepare a medium-hot indirect fire in your grill, with heat on one side and no heat on the other.

Arrange the shrimp in a disposable aluminum pan. Drizzle with the 2 tablespoons of olive oil, toss, and season with salt and pepper. Place the pan on the grill, close the lid, and grill for 2 to 3 minutes. Open the lid, stir the shrimp, and grill for 2 to 3 minutes more, or until all the shrimp are pink and opaque.

For the bruschetta, spread 1 side of each bread slice with about 1 teaspoon of the aïoli and adjust the seasonings to your taste. Grill the bread slices for 1 to 2 minutes per side, or until they have good grill marks. Serve the shrimp, bread, remaining aïoli, and relish on small plates.

CRISPY GRILLED BREAD, TANGY-SWEET GRILLED GRAPES, AND OOZY AGED cheese combine for a "give me more" appetizer or light meal. A combination of Cheddar and blue, such as Red Rock Cellar Aged Cheddar Blue from Minnesota, would be fabulous. Serve this with a glass (or two) of bubbly or a dry red wine, such as a pinot noir.

# GRILLED CIABATTA AND GRAPE CLUSTERS WITH PLANKED CHEDDAR AND PARMESAN

**MAKES 8 BRUSCHETTA**

1 (5-ounce) wedge aged Cheddar or Cheddar-blue cheese

1 (5-ounce) wedge Parmesan or Piave cheese

1 pound red seedless grapes on the stems, rinsed and patted dry

8 slices ciabatta

Extra-virgin olive oil for brushing

Soak a cedar or oak grilling or baking plank in water for at least 1 hour.

Prepare an indirect medium-hot fire in your grill, with heat on one side and no heat on the other.

Place the cheese wedges toward the middle of the prepared plank.

Place the plank, with its cheese, on the indirect side of the grill and close the lid. Plank for 15 to 20 minutes, or until the cheese is beginning to ooze. Let the plank sit on the no-heat side of the grill while you grill the grapes on the hot side, directly on the grill grates, turning often, until the grapes are scorched and blistered, about 4 minutes total. Brush the bread with olive oil and grill for 1 to 2 minutes per side, or until it has good grill marks. Snip the grapes into clusters and arrange around the cheese. Serve directly from the plank with a basket of the grilled ciabatta.

# FRESH SWEET CORN *AND* ZUCCHINI SALAD

**SERVES 4 TO 6**

You can make this raw salad several hours ahead of time and it will pickle itself into deliciousness. This was adapted from a recipe by food truck chef Venus Van Horn of Magical Meatball Tour in Kansas City.

———————— ≈ ————————

4 ears fresh sweet corn

2 medium-size zucchini, thinly sliced

1 finely chopped jalapeño pepper, seeded and membranes removed

¼ cup chopped fresh flat-leaf parsley

¼ cup freshly squeezed lime juice

¼ cup extra-virgin olive oil

Kosher or sea salt and freshly ground black pepper

Cut the kernels from the corn into a medium bowl. Toss with the zucchini, jalapeño pepper, and parsley. Pour the lime juice and olive oil into a jar, close the lid, and shake to blend. Pour the dressing over the salad and adjust the seasonings to your taste. Cover and keep at room temperature for 30 minutes or up to 8 hours, or until ready to serve.

HEARTY WINTER GREENS, SUCH AS BROCCOLI RABE, KALE, SWISS CHARD, and spinach, are interchangeable in this recipe. A quick sauté until the greens are wilted keeps the colors a brilliant dark green. The leaves and stems are tender and fragrantly laced with the thinly sliced garlic. Pile the greens, still dripping with olive oil, atop the toasted bread for an appetizer or delicious side with pasta or pizza.

# BROCCOLI RABE AND GARLIC BRUSCHETTA

MAKES 8
BRUSCHETTA

**For the sautéed broccoli rabe:**

8 ounces broccoli rabe, chopped

1 large garlic clove, thinly sliced

2 tablespoons extra-virgin olive oil

Pinch of red pepper flakes (less than ⅛ teaspoon)

⅛ teaspoon kosher or sea salt

**For the bruschetta:**

8 (½-inch-thick) slices Italian country bread

2 tablespoons extra-virgin olive oil

For the sautéed broccoli rabe, in a large skillet on the stovetop, heat 2 tablespoons of water and add the broccoli rabe and garlic. Cook until soft, 6 to 8 minutes. Drizzle with the olive oil and season with the red pepper flakes and salt. Adjust the seasonings to your taste, if needed.

For the bruschetta, prepare a medium-hot fire in your grill. Brush the bread with the olive oil and grill for 1 to 2 minutes per side, or until it has good grill marks.

Spoon a heaping tablespoon of the wilted broccoli rabe on each bruschetta and serve warm.

TOMATOES ARE THE FOCAL POINT OF SO MANY WONDERFUL TOPPING combinations. The mixtures can be naked or lightly dressed with a vinaigrette and topped or not with a shaving of cheese. If you're a tomato purist, simply top a charred piece of sourdough bruschetta with a juicy sliced off-the-vine tomato with a sprinkle of sea salt and drizzle of extra-virgin olive oil. When tomatoes and basil are at their peak, you'll want to devour two or three of these tangy sourdough bruschetta. See our Bruschetta Toppings sidebar (page 56) for more ideas.

## GARDEN TOMATO, BASIL, AND CAPER SOURDOUGH BRUSCHETTA

**MAKES 8 BRUSCHETTA**

8 slices artisan sourdough bread

10 Roma tomatoes, seeded and chopped

2 tablespoons capers, drained

8 to 12 large fresh basil leaves

Extra-virgin olive oil for drizzling

Coarse kosher or sea salt for sprinkling

Prepare a medium-hot fire in your grill.

Toast each slice of bread for 1 to 2 minutes per side, or until it has good grill marks.

In a large bowl, combine the tomatoes and capers. Roughly tear the basil leaves and stir into the mixture. Drizzle with olive oil and sprinkle with sea salt. Serve spooned on top of the grilled sourdough bread.

# Bruschetta Toppings

Start with rustic artisan loaves of ciabatta, Italian, caraway rye, sourdough, sesame semolina, Asiago cheese, pain de campagne, or other sturdy bakery bread. Slice the bread almost ½ inch thick so it can hold the toppings without falling apart. Grill the bread over the fire until it has good grill marks and is a medium golden brown. (If you're topping with cheese that needs to melt, set the bruschetta back onto the indirect side of the grill and close the lid for a couple of minutes.) Now the bruschetta is ready to top with any of the following toppings. A drizzle of really good extra-virgin olive oil is de rigueur on the savory toppings.

*White beans, garlic, and olive oil*

*Provolone cheese and prosciutto*

*Kalamata Olive Paste (page 104) and tomato*

*Avocado slices and freshly squeezed lemon juice*

*Grilled peppers, onions, and provolone cheese*

*Mozzarella cheese, tomato, and basil*

*Chive-Basil Pesto (page 144) and Pecorino Romano cheese*

*Grilled asparagus and feta cheese*

*Cream cheese, scrambled eggs, and snipped chives*

*Tomato, red onion, and bacon*

*Tuna, capers, and Parmesan Aïoli (page 57)*

*Barbecued pulled pork and goat cheese*

*Brie cheese, basil, and sun-dried tomatoes*

*Spinach Artichoke Dip (page 198)*

*Ricotta cheese and orange marmalade*

*Mascarpone and sliced strawberries or peaches*

*Goat cheese and fig preserves*

*Gorgonzola cheese and dark honey*

*Butter, cinnamon sugar, and fresh sliced fruit*

*Whipped cream cheese, sliced pears, sliced almonds, and honey*

*Chocolate hazelnut spread or dark chocolate and sea salt*

FOR A KICK-BACK, EMERIL-INSPIRED WEEKEND WHEN YOU WANT TO ENJOY life, serve this recipe. Make it your main course with a side platter of tomatoes or grilled vegetables. Your guests will gobble it all up. If you have a smaller gathering and don't want to invest in a whole tenderloin, buy a couple of beef fillets to grill and slice instead. Use Italian or semolina bread for the bruschetta.

# BIG EASY TENDERLOIN BRUSCHETTA WITH PARMESAN AÏOLI AND ARUGULA

SERVES 8 TO 10

**For the Parmesan aïoli:**

1 cup mayonnaise

½ cup Parmigiano-Reggiano cheese

2 tablespoons freshly squeezed lemon juice

1 garlic clove, minced

**For the beef tenderloin:**

4 pounds beef tenderloin, trimmed

Extra-virgin olive oil for brushing

Coarse kosher or sea salt and freshly ground black pepper

**For the bruschetta:**

1 loaf artisan bread, sliced ½ inch thick

4 to 5 cups baby arugula

4 ounces Parmigiano-Reggiano cheese, shaved with a vegetable peeler

Prepare a hot fire in your grill.

For the Parmesan aïoli, in a small bowl, combine the mayonnaise, Parmigiano-Reggiano, lemon juice, and garlic, stirring to blend. Refrigerate.

For the beef tenderloin, brush the tenderloin with olive oil and season with salt and pepper. Grill the tenderloin for 20 minutes with the lid down, turning it a quarter-turn every 5 minutes. Continue to turn and grill until an instant-read thermometer registers 130°F for rare or the meat is firm yet a little springy to the touch (or cooked to your desired doneness). Set aside to rest for 5 minutes.

For the bruschetta, over a medium-hot fire, grill each slice of bread for 1 to 2 minutes per side, or until it has good grill marks.

Slice the tenderloin about ¼ inch thick. Adjust the seasoning to your taste.

To assemble each bruschetta, spread some aïoli on the bread, place a slice of the tenderloin on top of the bread, top with some arugula and shaved Parmigiano-Reggiano, and eat while warm.

PREPARED POLENTA MAKES THIS RECIPE COME TOGETHER IN A SNAP. It's colorful, tasty, and only takes about 20 minutes to make. Polenta can be quite firm, but it can also be on the delicate side, so you may want to give everyone a small plate and fork to eat these.

# GRILLED POLENTA ROUNDS WITH SUN-DRIED TOMATOES

SERVES 4 TO 6

1 (16-ounce) package prepared polenta, cut into ½-inch-thick slices

Extra-virgin olive oil for brushing

1 cup sun-dried tomatoes packed in olive oil, lightly drained and slivered

1 garlic clove, minced

8 ounces feta cheese, crumbled

Several sprigs flat-leaf parsley for garnish

Prepare a medium-hot fire in your grill.

Brush the polenta slices with olive oil and place on a baking sheet.

In a small bowl, toss the sun-dried tomatoes with the garlic.

Place the polenta slices on the grill grates and grill for 2 to 3 minutes per side, turning once, until each side has good grill marks.

Arrange the grilled polenta on a platter. Spoon the tomato mixture over the polenta and top with the feta cheese. Garnish with the parsley.

**B**UTTERY BRIOCHE GRILLS QUICKLY TO A GOLDEN BROWN AND MAKES A delicious dessert bruschetta. A good-quality dark chocolate bar that's at least 45% cacao is best. If you like, choose a hazelnut chocolate bar for even more flavor. This grown-up version of s'mores begs for a bowl of juicy ripe strawberries to go with it.

# BRIOCHE BRUSCHETTA WITH DARK CHOCOLATE AND FLEUR DE SEL

**MAKES 16 SMALL BRUSCHETTA**

4 (¾-inch-thick) slices brioche

Extra-virgin olive oil for drizzling

1 (5- to 6-ounce) dark chocolate bar, broken into squares

Fleur de sel for sprinkling

Prepare an indirect medium-hot fire in your grill, with heat on one side and no heat on the other.

Place the brioche slices on a baking sheet and lightly drizzle the top side with the olive oil.

Grill the brioche slices for 1 to 2 minutes per side, until they have good grill marks and are golden brown. Remove from the grill.

Lay 4 squares of chocolate (arranged like a 4-pane square window) in the olive oil side of each grilled brioche slice. Place each brioche slice, chocolate-side up, on the indirect side of the grill and close the lid for a couple of minutes. Transfer to a cutting board and cut the bread into 4 squares. Lightly sprinkle with a pinch of fleur de sel and eat while warm.

**T**HIS IS A TERRIFIC TREAT THAT HAS SO MUCH STUNNING COLOR WHEN you use red and yellow raspberries. A rustic sourdough or ciabatta adds just enough savory contrast to the sweetened ricotta and sugared berries. Brioche or challah bread would be excellent for the bruschetta.

# RASPBERRY BRUSCHETTA WITH LAVENDER HONEY RICOTTA

**MAKES 4 BRUSCHETTA**

1 cup red raspberries

1 tablespoon granulated sugar, plus more as needed

1 cup ricotta cheese

3 tablespoons lavender honey, plus extra for drizzling

1 tablespoon freshly squeezed lemon juice

4 (¾-inch-thick) slices sourdough bread

2 tablespoons extra-virgin olive oil

1 cup yellow raspberries

4 small mint sprigs for garnish

Prepare a medium-hot fire in your grill.

Place ½ cup of the red raspberries in a bowl and mash with the sugar. Taste for sweetness and add more sugar, if needed.

In another bowl, combine the ricotta cheese with the lavender honey and lemon juice, whisking until smooth.

Lightly coat the sourdough bread with olive oil and grill for about 1 to 2 minutes per side, or until they have good grill marks.

On plates, slather each piece of bread with the ricotta mixture. Spoon some of the mashed red raspberries on top of the ricotta. Then arrange the remaining yellow and red raspberries on each bruschetta and top with a sprig of mint.

WHEN AUGUSTE ESCOFFIER WAS EXECUTIVE CHEF AT THE SAVOY IN London in the 1890s, he created Pêche Melba for Australian opera singer Nellie Melba. The combination of poached peaches, raspberry sauce, and vanilla ice cream has become a classic. Here, we've given it a spin on the grill, also with delicious results. In place of whipped cream on fruit desserts, we love honey-flavored Greek yogurt, especially the Greek Gods brand. But you can also stir honey into plain Greek yogurt.

# PEACH MELBA OPEN-FACE BRIOCHE

**MAKES 4 BRUSCHETTA**

4 ripe peaches, halved and pitted

2 tablespoons granulated sugar

Freshly squeezed lemon juice

4 (1-inch-thick) slices brioche loaf or challah

1 pint fresh raspberries

Honeyed Greek yogurt

Prepare a medium-hot fire in your grill.

Place the peach halves cut-side down on the grill. Grill for 4 to 6 minutes, turning once, until the peaches are tender and blistered.

Transfer the peaches to a work surface. Remove the skins, cut the peaches into thin slices, and place in a medium bowl. Sprinkle with sugar and a squeeze of lemon juice and toss to blend.

Grill the brioche slices for 1 to 2 minutes per side, or until they have good grill marks.

To serve, place each brioche slice on a plate and top with peaches, raspberries, and a dollop of honeyed Greek yogurt.

# Chapter 3

# SANDWICHES AND PANINI

———◇◇◇◇◇———

Why do savory sandwiches taste so much better when they're made at a pizzeria? It's the flavor from the toastiness of the bread and the meltiness of the cheese plus the high heat of the pizza oven. When you turn your grill into a pizza oven, you get even more flavor—the flavor of the grill.

We're spoiled by our choices of so many kinds of great bread these days, so experiment with your favorite artisan loaf and the grill techniques we give here to create your own custom sandwich.

We've expanded the idea of savory sandwiches and panini in this chapter to also include sweet dessert panini with chocolate and fresh fruit for the fillings. Brioche and challah take well to the high heat of the grill, toasting in mere minutes for easy, on-the-grill desserts.

Pizza oven–style sandwiches are great in warm weather but are also a great option when the weather turns brisk. Simply fire up the grill, put the sandwich on, close the lid, and sip a glass of wine while you stay toasty warm.

Heavy-duty aluminum foil, in some recipes, helps the sandwich ingredients ooze together deliciously while not making a mess on your grill. The foil also helps keep the bread from burning. If you're not sure how hot your grill is getting, just turn or move the sandwiches every few minutes or so.

For the panini, you'll need something heavy to press the sandwiches down on the grill. Although a heavy skillet works well, our favorite way to press the panini is with foil-wrapped bricks. A brick is the perfect size to place on top of a sandwich. Just use heavy-duty aluminum foil to wrap the clean bricks. Now you have your very own outdoor panini maker and it didn't cost you much.

WHEN JUDITH WAS IN HIGH SCHOOL, HER HOMETOWN ANGILO'S PIZZA served this pizza bread, beloved of starving teenagers and their frugal parents alike. This sandwich version of cheese pizza is simple, but the flavor of the grill will satisfy even the fussiest eater. With a fresh green salad, it makes a family-pleasing casual meal.

# PIZZA BREAD

**MAKES 4 HOAGIES**

4 (6-inch) hoagie rolls, split in half lengthwise

Extra-virgin olive oil for brushing

1 cup marinara or pizza sauce

2 cups grated provolone or mozzarella cheese

1 tablespoon dried Italian herb seasoning or a mixture of dried oregano, basil, and parsley

Prepare a medium-hot fire in your grill.

Brush the rolls on all sides with olive oil and place, cut-side up, in 2 disposable aluminum pans. Spread about 2 tablespoons of marinara sauce on each cut side. Sprinkle with the cheese and herbs.

Place the pans on the grill grates, close the lid, and grill for 5 to 6 minutes, or until the cheese has melted and the rolls are toasty. Put the sandwiches back together, gently press with your hands, cut in half, and serve hot.

**P**ARBOIL OR MICROWAVE THE BUTTERNUT SQUASH FIRST TO GIVE IT A HEAD start, then grill-roast to caramelize it to a tender finish. Serve this sandwich cut smaller for a nibble or cut larger for a meal.

# GRILL-ROASTED BUTTERNUT SQUASH, RED ONION, SAGE, AND RICOTTA LOAF
SERVES 4 TO 6

10 ounces butternut squash, peeled, seeded, and cut into 2-inch cubes (about 2 cups) and parcooked until almost tender

2 cups chopped red onion

Extra-virgin olive oil for brushing and drizzling

Coarse kosher or sea salt and freshly ground black pepper

24 fresh tender sage leaves

1 large round artisan loaf, such as Asiago, sourdough boule, or semolina

8 ounces ricotta cheese

Prepare a medium-hot fire in your grill.

Place the squash and red onion in a disposable aluminum pan, drizzle with olive oil, and season with salt and pepper. Place the pan on the grill grates, close the lid, and grill for 10 minutes, or until the squash is becoming tender and the onion begins to brown. Add the sage leaves and stir, close the lid, and grill for 5 to 10 more minutes, or until the herbs have roasted and the squash is tender when pierced with a fork.

Cut the Italian bread in half lengthwise and turn both halves cut-side up. With your fingers or a fork, hollow out about one-third of the top half of the bread and discard or reserve for another use. Brush the bottom half with more olive oil, then spread the ricotta cheese on it. Layer the grill-roasted squash mixture on top. Adjust the seasoning to taste. Brush the hollowed top half of the bread with olive oil and place on top of the sandwich fillings. Wrap well in heavy-duty aluminum foil.

Grill the loaf, covered, turning once, for 15 to 20 minutes, or until heated through. Slice and serve warm.

*Salad on the Side*

# MIXED GREENS WITH POMEGRANATE AND RICOTTA SALATA

**SERVES 4**

When pomegranates are in season from late fall to Valentine's Day, add their ruby red seeds to salads. Simply cut the pomegranate in half, and hold each half over a bowl and hit it with a wooden spoon so the seeds fall into the bowl. The mellow, yet salty taste of ricotta salata is a perfect foil to the other flavors. A simple dressing is all you need.

---

**4 cups baby greens**

**¼ cup thinly sliced red onion**

**1 tablespoon red wine vinegar**

**3 tablespoons extra-virgin olive oil**

**Coarse kosher or sea salt and freshly ground black pepper**

**¼ cup walnuts, toasted**

**½ cup freshly grated ricotta salata**

**½ cup fresh pomegranate seeds**

Place the greens and onion in a salad bowl. In a small bowl, whisk the vinegar and olive oil together. Adjust the seasoning to taste. Toss the salad with the dressing, then portion onto plates. Top each salad with walnuts, ricotta salata, and pomegranate seeds and serve.

P AN BAGNAT, OR "BATHED BREAD," IS THE MEDITERRANEAN'S VERSION OF a fast-food sandwich that you might buy at a Provençal food truck or beachside stand. Add a little American grilling to the mix, and you have a standout sandwich. Pan bagnat consists of crusty hard rolls or large baguettes doused with vinaigrette, piled high with summer vegetables, black olives, and tuna, and then pressed together so that all the juices permeate the sandwich. Grilled salmon fillet would also be delicious in this sandwich.

# GRILLED TUNA PAN BAGNAT

**MAKES 4 SANDWICHES**

1 large French baguette, cut in half lengthwise

2 (8-ounce) tuna steaks or salmon fillets

Extra-virgin olive oil for brushing

½ small red onion, finely chopped

½ cup chopped grape tomatoes

½ cup chopped, pitted oil-cured black olives, such as niçoise

¼ cup chopped fresh basil

2 tablespoons red wine vinegar

1 teaspoon Dijon mustard

1 teaspoon kosher or sea salt

½ teaspoon freshly ground black pepper

6 tablespoons olive oil

Prepare a medium-hot fire in your grill.

Brush the cut sides of the baguettes, then the tuna steaks, with olive oil. Grill the baguette, cut-side down, for 2 to 3 minutes, or until it has good grill marks. Grill the tuna for 3 to 4 minutes on each side, or until just cooked through. Let rest for 5 minutes. Flake the tuna with a fork into a medium bowl. Stir in the onion, tomatoes, olives, and basil. In a small bowl, whisk together the vinegar, mustard, salt, pepper, and olive oil. Pour the dressing over the tuna and mix gently to combine.

Spread the tuna mixture evenly over the bottom half of the bread, place the top half of the bread on top, and press down firmly on the sandwich. Wrap the sandwich in aluminum foil and place a heavy pan on top. Let stand 30 minutes at room temperature before serving and then cut into 4 pieces.

# GRILLED ENDIVE SALAD WITH DIJON VINAIGRETTE

## SERVES 4

Belgian endives are delicious with a dip and are easy to grill. Simply cut them in half lengthwise and grill before your sandwich or pizza. This knife-and-fork salad pairs well with a robust Dijon vinaigrette.

---

1 pound Belgian endive

Extra-virgin olive oil, as needed for brushing

Coarse kosher or sea salt and freshly ground black pepper

1 tablespoon freshly squeezed lemon juice

1 garlic clove, minced

1 teaspoon Dijon mustard

3 tablespoons olive oil

Snipped fresh flat-leaf parsley

Prepare a medium-hot fire in your grill.

Cut the Belgian endive in half lengthwise, rinse under cool running water, and pat dry. Brush with olive oil and season to taste. Grill the endive, cut-side down, until you have good grill marks, 3 to 4 minutes, then transfer to a serving platter.

In a bowl, whisk the lemon juice, garlic, mustard, and olive oil together until well blended. Adjust the seasoning to taste and drizzle over the endive. Sprinkle with parsley. Serve warm or at room temperature.

THE SAME INGREDIENTS THAT GO INTO A SUPREME PIZZA TASTE wonderful in a grilled sandwich that satisfies hearty appetites in brisk weather. The other virtue of this sandwich is that it can be made earlier in the day, wrapped, and refrigerated before grilling. Let it come to room temperature while you wait for the grill to warm up.

# PIZZA SANDWICH SUPREME

**SERVES 4 TO 6**

1 loaf Italian bread

Extra-virgin olive oil for brushing

2/3 cup marinara or pizza sauce

1/2 cup pepperoni slices

1/2 cup cooked, crumbled Italian or regular pork or turkey sausage

1/2 cup finely chopped red onion

1/2 cup seeded and finely chopped green bell pepper

1/2 cup pitted and sliced Kalamata olives

1 cup thinly sliced mushrooms (about 4 ounces)

2 cups shredded mozzarella or provolone cheese, or 8 slices

Prepare a medium-hot fire in your grill.

Cut the Italian bread in half lengthwise and turn both halves cut-side up. With your fingers or a fork, hollow out about one-third of the top half of the bread and discard or reserve for another use. Lightly brush the inside and outside of the bread with olive oil. Spread the bottom half with marinara sauce. Layer on the pepperoni, sausage, onion, bell pepper, olives, and mushrooms. Top with the cheese. Place the top half of the bread over the sandwich fillings. Wrap well in heavy-duty aluminum foil.

Grill, covered, turning once, for 20 to 25 minutes, or until heated through. Slice into individual servings.

A KAISER ROLL IS A MUST FOR THIS SANDWICH, WHICH REQUIRES A HE-MAN sturdy roll that can hold the weight of thick pulled pork. Make this all year round with pork butt that you slow-braised in the oven or slow-smoked on the grill. The pulled pork tastes great with the heat of red pepper flakes and an extra bit of vinegar added to your sauce. Grilling the pork as patties gives the meat a nice crispy texture. The pork holds together better if it is chilled for at least an hour. If you can't wait that long, then grill the pork patties on a grill rack or in a cast-iron skillet on the grill. A little dollop of Dijon mustard spread on the kaiser rolls adds extra zing to this sandwich. Top with Memphis-Style Coleslaw with 1-Minute Vinaigrette (page 137) for another extra punch of flavor.

# SPICY BBQ PULLED PORK ON A KAISER ROLL

SERVES 2

2 kaiser rolls

Extra-virgin olive oil
for brushing

1 pound cooked
and shredded pork butt

1 cup tomato-based
barbecue sauce

⅛ teaspoon red pepper flakes

2 tablespoons white
vinegar

2 tablespoons
Dijon mustard (optional)

Prepare a medium-hot fire in your grill. Place a skillet or grill rack on one side of the grill.

Brush the cut sides of the rolls with olive oil and set on a baking sheet.

In a bowl, pull the pork into small pieces. Add the barbecue sauce, red pepper flakes, and vinegar and toss to mix thoroughly. Form the meat into 2 large patties and refrigerate for at least 1 hour and up to 8 hours before grilling directly on the grill grates.

Grill the rolls, cut-side down, for 2 to 3 minutes, or until they have good grill marks. Grill the pork patties in the skillet or on the grill rack for 4 to 5 minutes on each side, or until just warmed through and crusty on the outside. Spread the mustard on the rolls, if you wish. Place a patty on the bottom half of each roll, top with the other half, slice in half, and serve at once.

SMOKED SALMON AND CREAM CHEESE IS A CLASSIC DUO GREAT FOR breakfast, lunch, or dinner. We've included a buttery croissant, which tastes delicious crisped up on the grill. Watercress is readily available at upscale grocery stores and adds a little radishlike sharpness to the smooth, velvety salmon and cream cheese. You could substitute baby spinach or arugula, or even nasturtium flowers and leaves for the watercress.

# SMOKED SALMON AND HERBED CREAM CHEESE ON GRILLED CROISSANTS

**MAKES 4 SANDWICHES**

4 ounces cream cheese, at room temperature

¼ cup chopped fresh herbs, such as chives, parsley, and dill

¼ cup finely chopped red onion

1 garlic clove, minced

4 large croissants, sliced in half lengthwise

4 ounces smoked salmon

1 cup watercress, red or regular

Prepare a medium-hot fire in your grill.

Combine the cream cheese, herbs, onion, and garlic and blend together. Spread the cream cheese mixture evenly over the 8 croissant halves. Place 1 ounce of salmon on each of the bottom croissant halves and top with ¼ cup of the watercress. Place the top of each croissant on top.

Place the croissants over the medium-hot fire. Set a foil-wrapped brick on top of each sandwich and grill for about 2 minutes. Remove the bricks and turn the sandwiches when they have good grill marks. Place the bricks on top of the sandwiches again and grill for another 2 minutes. Serve warm.

# Panini Combinations

Savory and sweet combinations for panini are limitless. Set up a panini bar of different ingredients and encourage people to make their own unique combinations. The meats and cheeses are always better if thinly sliced.

*Ham and Emmentaler or fontina cheese with grainy mustard*

*Turkey, Brie cheese, and basil*

*Mushrooms, caramelized onions, and fontina cheese*

*Grilled eggplant, marinara sauce, and mozzarella cheese*

*Grilled chicken, mozzarella cheese, and sun-dried tomato*

*Grilled asparagus and Goat Cheese-Olive-Lemon Spread (page 193)*

*Salami, Havarti cheese, and Roasted Red Pepper Sauce (page 191)*

*Prosciutto, Gruyère cheese, fresh spinach, and caramelized onions*

*Avocado, bacon, and pepper Jack cheese*

*Asparagus, feta cheese, and lemon zest*

*Corned beef and cabbage Reuben with Thousand Island dressing*

*Grilled salmon with sliced avocado and crispy bacon*

*Smoked Gouda cheese, apple, and ham*

*Tapenade, tomato, and provolone cheese*

*Olive muffalata with thin Italian meats and cheeses*

*Bratwurst and sauerkraut on rye*

*Chicken, bacon, and avocado with Chive-Basil Pesto (page 144)*

*Mozzarella cheese with tomato spoon jam*

*Goat Cheese-Olive-Lemon Spread (page 193) and sun-dried tomatoes*

*Mascarpone, fig preserves, and honey*

*Chocolate hazelnut spread*

*Almond butter and apricot preserves*

GATHER FRIENDS TOGETHER AND TRY THESE WHOLE-LOAF PANINI FOR A casual evening on the deck or patio. Assemble a couple of these sandwiches ahead of time and finish on the grill when you are ready to serve them crunchy, toasty, gooey, and warm. Add a big leafy green salad and glasses of crisp pinot grigio, and you've got dinner.

# GRILLED CHICKEN PESTO PANINI
## WITH AVOCADO AND BACON

MAKES 6
PANINI

1 pound chicken tenders

Extra-virgin olive oil
for brushing

Kosher or sea salt and
freshly ground black pepper

1 large, long loaf French
or Italian bread

1/2 cup store-bought
pesto or Chive-Basil Pesto
(page 144)

1/4 cup mayonnaise

1 avocado, peeled, pitted,
and sliced

6 strips cooked bacon

1 cup shredded Monterey
Jack cheese

Prepare a medium-hot fire in your grill.

Lightly coat the chicken tenders with olive oil and season with salt and pepper. Grill the chicken directly over the fire for 2 to 3 minutes per side, turning once. Set aside.

Slice the loaf of bread in half lengthwise and lightly brush all sides with olive oil. Spread the pesto on one cut side and the mayonnaise on the other. Layer the grilled chicken tenders, slices of avocado, bacon, and cheese evenly over all and place the bread lid on top.

Place the panino directly over the fire and set 2 or 3 foil-wrapped bricks on top of the bread to weigh it down. You may need to push the bricks to lightly smash the sandwich. Grill for about 2 minutes, until it's toasty with good grill marks, then turn it over and grill for about the same amount of time. Set the panino on a cutting board and let rest for 2 to 3 minutes. Then slice at a diagonal into 6 portions, using a good bread knife.

SOFT BREADS, SUCH AS BRIOCHE AND SEMOLINA, ARE PERFECT FOR DESSERT panini. Other interesting breads would be walnut bread or fruit-studded bread from artisan bakeries. These denser breads need to be sliced thinly so they don't overwhelm the sandwich. We like to cut the crusts off the bread and slice the sandwiches on the diagonal. These sweet treats would be perfect served with a cup of coffee or tea for brunch or dessert.

# HONEYED GOAT CHEESE AND APRICOT PANINI

MAKES 4
PANINI

8 (1-inch-thick) slices brioche or (1/2-inch-thick) slices fruit- or nut-studded bread, crusts removed

4 tablespoons (1/2 stick) butter, at room temperature

6 ounces goat cheese

6 tablespoons apricot preserves

8 dried apricots, chopped

4 teaspoons wildflower or dark honey

Prepare a medium-hot fire in your grill.

Lightly butter one side of each bread slice and lay, buttered-side down, on a baking sheet. Spread 1½ ounces of the goat cheese on 4 of the slices and 1½ tablespoons of apricot jam on the other 4 slices. Sprinkle one-quarter of the chopped dried apricots over the goat cheese and drizzle each with 1 teaspoon of honey. Place the jam side of the bread on top of the goat cheese to make 4 sandwiches.

Place the sandwiches over the medium-hot fire. Set a foil-wrapped brick on top of each sandwich and grill for about 2 minutes. Remove the bricks and turn the sandwiches if they have good grill marks. Place the bricks on top of the sandwiches again and grill for another 2 minutes. Cut the sandwiches on the diagonal and serve warm.

**B**ECAUSE FOCACCIA COMES IN ALL DIFFERENT SIZES, IT'S HARD TO SPECIFY a size, so just use enough for four sandwiches according to your appetite. *Al mattone* refers to a brick, which is used to press down the panini as they grill (see page 66).

# PROSCIUTTO, PROVOLONE, AND ROASTED RED PEPPER PANINI AL MATTONE

MAKES 4
PANINI

4 squares focaccia, sliced in half horizontally

Extra-virgin olive oil for brushing

8 slices provolone cheese

2 roasted red peppers, halved

8 thin slices prosciutto

Prepare a medium-hot fire in your grill.

Brush all sides of each focaccia slice with olive oil. On the bottom portion of each sandwich, place 2 slices of cheese, then a pepper half, then 2 slices of prosciutto. Top with the remaining focaccia slices. Place the panini on a baking sheet to take out to the grill.

Place each panino on the grill rack and weight with a foil-wrapped brick. Grill for 3 to 4 minutes on each side, or until it has good grill marks and the cheese has melted. Slice each panino in half and serve hot.

**K**AREN'S MOTHER MAKES THE BEST PIES AND JAMS. EVERY SUMMER THEY would pick sour cherries from a tree in their neighbor Mrs. Brownfield's yard. Karen and her mother would pit the cherries at home and make a double-crust, lattice-topped cherry pie. This dessert panini catches the essence of those same flavors. You can make your own jam or buy a good jar. The optional pickled jalapeños add a nice little kick to offset the sweetness of the mascarpone and sweet jam.

# DESSERT PANINI WITH MASCARPONE AND SOUR CHERRIES

MAKES 4
PANINI

8 (1-inch-thick) slices brioche, crusts removed

4 tablespoons (½ stick) butter, at room temperature

½ cup mascarpone

½ cup sour cherry jam or preserves

4 teaspoons chopped pickled jalapeño pepper (optional)

Prepare a medium-hot fire in your grill.

Lightly butter one side of each bread slice and lay, buttered-side down, on a baking sheet. Spread 2 tablespoons of mascarpone on 4 of the slices and 2 tablespoons of cherry jam on the other 4 slices. If you would like a little heat, sprinkle 1 teaspoon of pickled jalapeño over the mascarpone. Place the cherry jam side of the bread on top of the mascarpone to make 4 sandwiches.

Place the sandwiches over the medium-hot fire. Set a foil-wrapped brick on top of each sandwich and grill for about 2 minutes. Remove the bricks and turn the sandwiches if they have good grill marks. Place the bricks on top of the sandwiches again and grill for another 2 minutes. Cut the sandwiches on the diagonal and serve warm.

# Chapter 4

## FLATBREADS AND FOCACCIA

———◦◦◇◇◦◦———

Whoever first mixed up dough, flattened it out, and cooked it over an open fire was simply brilliant. So brilliant that the idea spread all over the world, across time and cultures. From Afghan naan cooked against the sides of a ceramic tandoor to fatir grilled on a Big Green Egg in an Atlanta backyard, fire and flatbread is a great combination.

In this chapter, we'll explore the flatbreads of the Mediterranean and beyond that work well on the grill grates of a gas or charcoal grill. The Black Sesame Flatbread with Miso-Laced Cream Cheese (page 97), Lebanese Flatbread with Feta, Za'atar, and Chives (page 99), and Grilled Garlic and Herb Breadsticks with Garlic and Herb Butter (page 102) give you a little taste preview.

Stir up a dough and let it rise. (Allow about 1 hour, or prepare up to 2 days ahead, let rise, cover, refrigerate, and bring back to room temperature before using.)

Transfer the dough to a floured surface (or an oiled surface for gluten-free dough). At this point, you can roll the dough in extra flavorings, such as sesame seeds, dried herbs, spices, and crumbled or grated cheeses. Then, cut off portions of dough, brush both sides with olive oil, and grill.

Our yeast doughs perform on the grill as a pancake does on a griddle. When you place a portion of dough on the hot grill grate, it will bubble up. When the underside has browned—in a minute or two—and solidifies (also, just like a pancake), you can turn the flatbread with tongs or a spatula, add any topping, and grill the other side. You can also add a kiss of smoke (see page 21) during the grilling process, for an additional smoky flavor.

A great recipe to start off with is the Simple Grilled Flatbread with Fresh Herbs and Romano (page 90). This will get you used to the technique of grilling directly over the heat source. Then, you can create your own signature flatbreads on the grill.

We also have recipes for preparing a thicker flatbread or focaccia in an aluminum pan, which is grilled indirectly. This allows you to load the dough with lots of goodies, almost like a deep-dish pizza. Cornmeal is sprinkled onto the bottom of the pan to prevent sticking. (Don't use oil—it gets so hot that it causes the dough to burn on the bottom. We've done that!) Indirect grilling works best. If you don't think you have indirect capability on your grill, simply raise the pan above the heat by placing two or three bricks on top of the grill grates. Begin with the easy recipe for Basic Grilled Rosemary Focaccia (page 104).

Flavorful ingredients can also be added to the flatbread dough as you are making it. Flavored Focaccia Dough (see page 103) gives you a list of ingredients to add to the dough, such as olives, sun-dried tomatoes, dried fruits, and more. These thicker flavored flatbreads are decadent as sandwich or panini bread sliced horizontally and then layered with the cheeses, veggies, or meats of your choice.

**I**F YOU'RE WONDERING JUST HOW GOOD A FLATBREAD CAN TASTE, THIS recipe will convince you. For a gluten-free version, use Herbed Gluten-Free Pizza Dough (page 36).

# SIMPLE GRILLED FLATBREAD WITH FRESH HERBS AND ROMANO

SERVES 4

1 recipe Stir-Together
Flatbread Dough (page 32) or
Herbed Gluten-Free
Pizza Dough (page 36)

All-purpose flour
for dusting (optional)

Extra-virgin olive oil
for oiling (optional) and
brushing

½ cup grated Pecorino
Romano cheese

1 cup snipped mixed
fresh herbs, such as chives,
flat-leaf parsley, oregano,
and basil

Prepare a medium-hot fire in your grill.

For the Stir-Together Flatbread Dough, transfer the dough to a floured surface, and divide into quarters. Flour a rolling pin or your hands and roll or pat each portion of dough into an oval 8 inches long and ¼ inch thick.

For the Herbed Gluten-Free Pizza Dough, oil a work surface and your hands and divide the dough into quarters. Roll or pat each portion of dough into an oval 8 inches long and ¼ inch thick.

Brush the top and bottom side of each dough oval with olive oil. Grill over direct medium-high heat until you see the dough starting to bubble like a pancake, 2 to 3 minutes, and the bottoms have good grill marks. Turn and grill for 1 more minute, or until the other side has good grill marks. Sprinkle with the Pecorino Romano, top with the fresh herbs, and serve hot.

# Flatbreads Around the World

Many cultures have signature flatbreads that used to be cooked in the dying embers of a fire, on a hot stone over a fire, or twisted around a stick over a fire. Many of these have moved to the more modern technology of a wood-fired outdoor oven. Made in smaller, more manageable shapes, they can also be grilled directly on the grill grates.

| Flatbread | Country | Cooking Method |
| --- | --- | --- |
| Torta sul Testo | Italy | Hot stone or griddle over a fire |
| Damper | Australia | Dough twisted around a stick over a fire |
| Coca | Spain | Wood-fired grill or oven |
| Fatir | Egypt, Saudi Arabia | Wood-fired oven |
| Gozlem | Turkey | Oiled metal plate on a charcoal grill |
| Mana'eesh | Lebanon, Palestine, Syria | Wood-fired oven or charcoal grill |
| Msemmen | Algeria | Oiled metal plate on a charcoal grill |
| Naan | India, Pakistan, Afghanistan | Ceramic tandoor or charcoal grill |
| Pissaladière | France | Wood-fired oven |

FLATBREADS CAN ALSO TAKE A SWEET TURN. ON A COOL SPRING OR AUTUMN night, sit under the stars and let the honey drip from your chin. You'll want whole cardamom pods to crush and grind yourself to get the best aroma and flavor. You can find green cardamom in the pod at Middle Eastern markets, herb and spice shops, and natural food stores. If you can't find cardamom, then substitute ½ teaspoon of ground cinnamon. Lavender-colored chive blossoms provide a beautiful, edible garnish.

# TURKISH GRILLED FLATBREAD
## WITH HONEY, PISTACHIOS, AND CARDAMOM        SERVES 8

½ cup wildflower, clover, or other amber-colored honey

5 green cardamom pods

½ cup shelled, roughly chopped pistachios

1 recipe Stir-Together Flatbread Dough (page 32)

All-purpose flour for dusting

Extra-virgin olive oil for brushing

Chive blossoms for garnish

Prepare a medium-hot fire in your grill. Pour the honey into a bowl.

With a paring knife, slit open the cardamom pods, and pick off and discard the pods. Transfer the seeds to a spice grinder and grind finely.

For the Stir-Together Flatbread Dough, transfer the dough to a floured surface and cut into 8 pieces. Flour a rolling pin or your hands and roll or pat each piece into an oval 4 inches long and ¼ inch thick.

Brush the top and bottom side of each dough oval with olive oil. Grill over direct medium-high heat until you see the dough starting to bubble like a pancake, 2 to 3 minutes, and the bottoms have good grill marks. Turn and grill for 1 more minute, or until the other side has good grill marks. Drizzle with honey. Sprinkle with the ground cardamom and pistachios. Garnish with chive blossoms and serve hot with plenty of napkins.

**K**NOWN AS *MSEMMEN*, THIS WHOLE WHEAT FLATBREAD WITH ITS INTERIOR swirls of flavored oil can be cooked on an oiled grill griddle or directly on the grill grates. Serve this with chicken tagine or grilled chicken kebabs.

# GRILLED ALGERIAN SPICE-SWIRLED FLATBREAD

SERVES 8

1 recipe Whole Wheat Pizza Dough (page 34)

All-purpose flour for dusting

1 teaspoon salt

¼ cup olive oil, plus more for brushing

1 teaspoon ground cumin

1 teaspoon sweet paprika

1 teaspoon ground turmeric

Prepare a medium-hot fire in your grill.

Transfer the dough to a floured surface and press or roll into an 18 x 14-inch rectangle, ¼ inch thick. In a small bowl, combine the salt, olive oil, 1½ cups of water, and the cumin, paprika, and turmeric. Brush this mixture over the dough. Starting from a long end, roll up the dough into a tight cylinder. Cut the cylinder into 16 rolls. Press or roll each roll into a round ½ inch thick and 4 inches wide. Brush the tops with olive oil and grill directly on the grill grates for 3 to 4 minutes, or until the underside has good grill marks. Turn the flatbreads and grill the bottoms for another 1 to 2 minutes, or until done. Serve hot.

# FARMERS' MARKET SALAD

**SERVES 10 TO 12**

Once you get the gist of this farm fresh vegetable salad, you can make it your own with your choice of fresh vegetables from your garden or the market. The vegetables can be sliced thinly or chopped into chunks; let your time and mood guide you. This salad makes a lot but keeps for another day refrigerated. It's great with pizza, panini, bruschetta, focaccia, or just about anything grilled.

⟨≈⟩

10 ripe Roma tomatoes (about 1½ pounds), sliced into wedges

1 cucumber, chopped

2 ribs celery, chopped

1 red bell pepper, cored, seeded, and chopped

1 yellow bell pepper, cored, seeded, and chopped

1 red onion, peeled and slivered

1 (8-ounce) can artichoke hearts, drained and chopped

1 cup olives, pitted and halved

10 capers, drained

10 pepperoncini

3 garlic cloves, chopped or thinly sliced

8 to 10 large fresh basil leaves, torn

2 tablespoons roughly chopped fresh flat-leaf parsley

1 teaspoon finely chopped fresh rosemary

Zest and juice of 1 lemon

Extra-virgin olive oil for drizzling

Kosher or sea salt and freshly ground black pepper

In a large bowl, combine the tomatoes, cucumber, celery, peppers, onion, artichoke hearts, olives, capers, pepperoncini, garlic, basil, parsley, and rosemary. Add the lemon zest and juice, drizzle with olive oil, and stir. Adjust the seasonings to taste. Let sit for at least 30 minutes and up to 2 hours before serving.

JUST A LITTLE TWEAK TO THE BASIC GRILLED FLATBREAD RECIPE PAYS BIg taste dividends. First, make the miso-flavored cream cheese; it develops deeper flavors as it sits, so you can make it up to 5 days before serving. Miso, a fermented soy paste available in the refrigerated section of the grocery store, has an umami flavor similar to Worcestershire sauce. For a vegan version, use vegan cream cheese. Then, roll black sesame seeds into the dough after it has risen. Serve these flatbreads hot with the cream cheese spread and maybe slices of grilled Japanese eggplant or rounds of fresh cucumber.

# BLACK SESAME FLATBREAD
# WITH MISO-LACED CREAM CHEESE

SERVES 4

### For the miso-laced cream cheese:

1 (8-ounce) package cream cheese, at room temperature

3 tablespoons brown miso, or more to taste

3 tablespoons mirin (Japanese rice wine)

2 tablespoons finely chopped green onion for garnish

### For the flatbread:

1 recipe Stir-Together Flatbread Dough (page 32) or Classic Pizza Dough (page 33)

All-purpose flour for dusting

2 tablespoons black sesame seeds

Extra-virgin olive oil for brushing

For the miso-laced cream cheese, place the cream cheese, miso, and mirin in a food processor and process until smooth. Serve immediately or cover and refrigerate for up to 5 days before serving. Let come to room temperature before serving.

*(recipe continues)*

For the flatbread, prepare a medium-hot fire in your grill.

Transfer the dough to a floured surface and pat into a large oval 12 inches long and ½ inch thick. Sprinkle the dough with half of the sesame seeds, gently pressing the seeds into the surface. Flour a rolling pin. Fold the dough in half and roll out to an oval 12 inches long and ½ inch thick. Sprinkle the remaining seeds over the dough, and repeat the process. The seeds should be dispersed throughout the dough. Divide the dough into quarters. Flour a rolling pin or your hands and roll or pat each portion of dough into an oval 8 inches long and ¼ inch thick.

Brush the top and bottom side of each dough oval with olive oil. Grill over direct medium-high heat until you see the dough starting to bubble like a pancake, 2 to 3 minutes, and the bottoms have good grill marks. Turn and grill for 1 more minute, or until the other side has good grill marks. Serve hot with the miso-laced cream cheese, garnished with green onion.

A DAPTED FROM A RECIPE BY FAMED LONDON CHEF YOTAM OTTOLENGHI, this flavorful flatbread just needs a drizzle of olive oil to finish. This take on mana'eesh, a breakfast flatbread in Syria and Lebanon, is great for meze ("little plates," or Middle Eastern–style appetizers). Serve this with cured olives, cucumber, and cherry tomatoes. Za'atar is a spice blend consisting of citrus-flavored dried sumac, toasted sesame seeds, dried thyme, and marjoram; it is available at Middle Eastern markets or from online spice houses, such as Penzeys.

# LEBANESE FLATBREAD
# WITH FETA, ZA'ATAR, AND CHIVES

SERVES 4

### For the feta, za'atar, and chive filling:

1 cup grated mozzarella cheese

1/4 cup crumbled feta cheese

2 tablespoons snipped fresh chives

1/4 teaspoon dried thyme

2 teaspoons za'atar

### For the flatbread:

1 recipe Stir-Together Flatbread Dough (page 32) or Classic Pizza Dough (page 33)

All-purpose flour for dusting

Extra-virgin olive oil for brushing

Prepare a medium-hot fire in your grill.

For the feta, za'atar, and chive filling, mix the mozzarella, feta, chives, thyme, and za'atar together in a bowl.

For the flatbread, transfer the dough to a floured surface and pat into a large oval 12 inches long and 1/2 inch thick. Sprinkle the dough with half of the filling, gently pressing the mixture into the surface. Flour a rolling pin. Fold the dough in half and roll out to a large oval 12 inches long and 1/2 inch thick. Spoon the remaining filling over the dough, and repeat the process. Roll the dough into a 16 x 6-inch rectangle, 1/2 inch thick. The filling should be dispersed throughout the dough. Using a sharp knife or a pizza cutter cut the dough into 2-inch x 5- to 6-inch pieces.

Brush the top and bottom side of each piece with olive oil. Place each piece perpendicular to the grill grate

*(recipe continues)*

so they don't fall through or grill on an oiled, perforated grill rack. Grill over direct medium-high heat until you see the dough starting to bubble like a pancake, 2 to 3 minutes, and the bottoms have good grill marks. Turn and grill for 1 more minute, or until the other side has good grill marks. Serve hot.

# ONION, CUCUMBER, AND TOMATO RAITA

**SERVES 4**

An Indian-style yogurt dipping sauce becomes a side salad, with the addition of these crisp garden fresh vegetables. It's perfect to serve with flatbread and still juicy enough for dipping.

---

½ cup chopped green onion

1 cucumber, seeded and chopped

1 large tomato, peeled, seeded, and chopped

2 jalapeño peppers, seeded and diced

2 tablespoons chopped fresh cilantro

1½ cups plain yogurt (not fat-free)

Combine all the ingredients and serve at room temperature, or chill the salad for an hour before serving.

O H, MY! MAKE TWO BOWLS OF DOUGH AND TWO BATCHES OF FLAVORED butter, because these will go fast. Served with a platter of grilled vegetables or a great steak, these breadsticks are as good as you can imagine. If you're concerned about having the breadsticks fall through the grill grates, simply grill them on an oiled, perforated grill rack (though laying them on the grill perpendicular to the grates should keep them from falling through). The butter will keep, refrigerated, for about a week. Frozen, the butter will keep for about 3 months (wrap in freezer plastic or paper).

# GRILLED GARLIC AND HERB BREADSTICKS WITH GARLIC HERB BUTTER

SERVES 4

**For the garlic and herb butter:**

4 ounces (1 stick) unsalted butter, at room temperature

½ cup chopped mixed fresh herbs, such as basil, chives, flat-leaf parsley, and dill

1 garlic clove, minced

¼ teaspoon salt, or more to taste

**For the breadsticks:**

1 recipe Garlic and Herb Pizza Dough (page 33)

All-purpose flour for dusting

Extra-virgin olive oil for brushing

Prepare a medium-hot fire in your grill.

For the garlic and herb butter, combine the butter, herbs, garlic and salt in a bowl and blend well with a fork. Cover with plastic wrap.

For the breadsticks, transfer the dough to a floured surface. Flour a rolling pin and roll into a 16 x 6-inch rectangle, ½ inch thick. Using a sharp knife or a pizza cutter, cut the dough into 2-inch x 5- to 6-inch pieces. Brush the top and bottom side of each piece with olive oil. Place each piece perpendicular to the grill grate so they don't fall through or grill on an oiled, perforated grill rack. Grill over direct medium-high heat until you see the dough starting to bubble like a pancake, 2 to 3 minutes, and the bottoms have good grill marks. Turn and grill for 1 more minute, or until the other side has good grill marks. Serve hot with the garlic and herb butter.

# Flavored Focaccia Dough and Toppings

Not only does the addition of olives, sun-dried tomatoes, hot peppers, cubes of cheese, dried fruits, garlic, and chopped herbs add flavor to flatbread dough, but the dough also can take on the color of the added ingredients, which adds aesthetic appeal as well as flavor.

The addition of these ingredients is simple. As you make the Stir-Together Flatbread Dough (page 32), stir in the additional ingredients and let rise according to the recipe instructions (page 33). Because such extras as olives, cheese, and dried fruits have weight, you may add 1 or 2 teaspoons more of the yeast, but it isn't mandatory.

**Flavored Focaccia Dough:**

Sun-Dried Tomato Dough: Add ¼ cup (or more) of chopped sun-dried tomatoes.

Roquefort and Walnut Dough: Add 1 cup of crumbled Roquefort cheese and ½ cup of toasted walnuts.

Dried Fruit Dough: Add ½ cup of chopped dried apricots or other dried fruits of your choice.

Fresh Herb Dough: Add 1 cup of chopped fresh herbs of your choice, such as sage, chives, thyme, oregano, or rosemary, or a mixture of them.

Cheese Dough: Add 1 cup of grated, cubed, or crumbled Asiago, Romano, Parmesan, Cheddar, Gorgonzola, or cheese of your choice (for double cheese, top the focaccia with additional cheese during grill-baking).

Meat-Studded Dough: Add 1 cup of diced prosciutto, salami, or other Italian deli sausages, cooked bacon crumbles, or diced cooked pancetta.

THIS RECIPE IS THE PERFECT BEGINNER'S FOCACCIA. IT'S SIMPLE, EASY, and allows you to taste the wonderful dough with very little accoutrements. We s uggest that the olive paste be served on the side. A tip we learned is to add softened butter to the olive paste to tame it down if it's too strong for your palate. Because the bread dough is soft and thick and the toppings are placed on the dough at the beginning, we use an aluminum pan to hold it together and to grill-bake it.

# BASIC GRILLED ROSEMARY FOCACCIA
# WITH KALAMATA OLIVE PASTE                    SERVES 8

**For the flatbread:**

1 teaspoon cornmeal

1 recipe Stir-Together Flatbread Dough (page 32)

Extra-virgin olive oil for brushing and drizzling

1 (6- to 8-inch) sprig tender, fresh rosemary

½ teaspoon coarse sea salt

**For the Kalamata olive paste:**

1 cup finely chopped Kalamata olives or other strongly flavored olives

2 tablespoons extra-virgin olive oil

Zest and juice of 1 lemon

2 tablespoons butter, at room temperature (optional)

Prepare an indirect medium-hot fire in your grill, with heat on one side and no heat on the other.

For the flatbread, lightly sprinkle the cornmeal in the bottom of a 12 x 10-inch disposable aluminum pan.

Dollop the dough down the center of the prepared pan. Dip your fingers in olive oil and carefully spread the dough to the edges of the pan so that the dough is an even thickness throughout. Lightly make some indentations all over the dough.

Sprinkle the rosemary leaves evenly over the dough, drizzle with olive oil, and sprinkle with the salt.

Set the pan on the indirect side of the grill or on top of 2 or 3 bricks placed on the grill grates to elevate the focaccia. Grill for 15 to 18 minutes with the lid closed. Check to see that the middle of the dough is 190°F.

For the Kalamata olive paste, while the bread is grill-baking, combine the olives, olive oil, and lemon zest and juice in a medium bowl. Stir in the butter, if you like. This can also be made in a food processor, but don't overblend.

THE SWEET FRESH FIG AND PUNGENT BLUE CHEESE MEET A MELLOW DOUGH that gets a bit of bitter char from the grill. Heaven. Just stand around and wolf these down as soon as they come off the grill grates. You'll be glad you did.

# GRILLED FRESH FIG AND GORGONZOLA FLATBREADS

MAKES 8
SMALL FLATBREADS

1 recipe Stir-Together
Flatbread Dough (page 32)

All-purpose flour
for dusting

2 fresh, ripe figs, cut
into ½-inch slices

4 ounces crumbled
Gorgonzola cheese

Extra-virgin olive oil
for brushing

Prepare a medium-hot fire in your grill.

Transfer the dough to a floured surface and cut into 8 equal pieces. Flour a rolling pin. Roll each piece into a 5 x 3-inch oval, ¼-inch thick. Place 2 fig slices and a table-spoon of Gorgonzola in the center of the oval. Fold the dough in half, stretching it a little to form it into a half-moon. Pinch the edges closed. Repeat the process with the remaining dough pieces, figs, and Gorgonzola.

Brush the top and bottom side of each stuffed flat-bread with olive oil. Grill over direct medium-high heat until you see the dough starting to bubble like a pancake, 2 to 3 minutes, and the bottoms have good grill marks. Turn and grill for 1 more minute, or until the other side has good grill marks. Serve hot.

**T**HIS IS A SLIGHT VARIATION ON HOW TO ADD INGREDIENTS TO THE DOUGH. Instead of dumping the ingredients into the dough as you stir it together, fold them into the dough while working with it on a floured board.

# PEPPER JACK, JALAPEÑO, AND ROASTED RED PEPPER–FILLED FLATBREAD
SERVES 8

1 teaspoon cornmeal

1 recipe Stir-Together Flatbread Dough (page 32)

All-purpose flour for dusting

1 cup pepper Jack cheese, cut into 1/2-inch cubes

2 jalapeño peppers, seeded and sliced

1 roasted red bell pepper, chopped

Extra-virgin olive oil for brushing and drizzling

1/2 teaspoon coarse sea salt

Lightly sprinkle the cornmeal in the bottom of a 12 x 10-inch disposable aluminum pan.

Place the dough on a lightly floured board and lightly sprinkle with flour. Stretch the dough to a rectangle and scatter half of the cheese, jalapeño, and red pepper on top. Fold the dough in half and set in the prepared pan. Dip your fingers in olive oil and carefully spread the dough to the edges of the pan so that the dough is an even thickness throughout. Lightly make some indentations and scatter the rest of the cheese, jalapeño, and red pepper on top, pressing lightly into the dough. Drizzle with olive oil and sprinkle with the salt. Let rest for 30 minutes covered with plastic wrap or a damp kitchen towel.

Prepare an indirect medium-hot fire in your grill, with heat on one side and no heat on the other.

Set the pan on the indirect side of the grill or on top of 2 or 3 bricks placed on the grill grates to elevate the focaccia. Grill for 25 to 30 minutes with the lid closed. Check to see that the middle of the dough is 190°F.

THIS TAKES FLATBREAD A STEP FURTHER BY MAKING IT INTO A SANDWICH. This is somewhat similar to the Panuozzo alla Pancetta (page 222), but made with softer dough and grilled over medium-high heat, rather than the pizza dough version of the panuozzo, which is grilled over high heat. The fillings for either sandwich could be mixed and matched to suit your tastes.

# OLIVE-STUDDED FLATBREAD STUFFED WITH APRICOT, PROSCIUTTO, AND PROVOLONE

SERVES 4

1 teaspoon cornmeal

1 recipe Stir-Together Flatbread Dough (page 32), prepared with the addition of 1 cup pitted and halved Kalamata olives

Extra-virgin olive oil for brushing and drizzling

1/2 teaspoon coarse sea salt

1/3 cup apricot preserves

6 slices prosciutto

4 slices provolone cheese

Prepare an indirect medium-hot fire in your grill, with heat on one side and no heat on the other.

Lightly sprinkle the cornmeal in the bottom of a 12 x 10-inch disposable aluminum pan.

Dollop the dough down the center of the prepared pan. Drizzle lightly with olive oil and carefully spread the dough to a 10-inch square with an even thickness throughout. Lightly make some indentations, drizzle lightly with more olive oil, if needed, and sprinkle with the salt.

Set the pan on the indirect side of the grill or on top of 2 or 3 bricks placed on the grill grates to elevate the focaccia. Grill for about 20 minutes with the lid closed. It's done when a thermometer inserted into the middle of the bread registers 190°F.

Remove from the grill and turn the bread onto a cutting board. Using a kitchen towel to protect your hands, cut the bread horizontally with a bread or serrated knife to make two thin layers. Brush the insides lightly with olive oil and spread the apricot preserves on the bottom half. Top with the prosciutto, provolone, and top half of the bread and wrap loosely in aluminum foil. Place back on the grill directly on top of the bricks for about 5 more minutes, to melt the cheese. Slice into quarters and serve at once.

TUSCANS HAVE THEIR OWN TERM FOR FOCACCIA—*SCHIACCIATA*—WHICH means "flattened down" or "squished." It is traditionally found in bakeries at grape harvest time and is made with the Sangiovese grapes dusted with sugar. This version uses a two-color mix of grapes, but other wine grapes could be used, as could blackberries, blueberries, or even raisins. Top it with honeyed whipped cream and sip a glass of Vin Santo or other dessert wine.

# TUSCAN SCHIACCIATA
# <u>WITH</u> BLACK AND PURPLE GRAPES

SERVES 6 TO 8

1 teaspoon cornmeal

1 recipe Stir-Together Flatbread Dough (page 32)

Extra-virgin olive oil for drizzling

1 cup seedless black grapes

1 cup seedless red grapes

¾ cup dark brown sugar

½ teaspoon coarse sea salt

For the honeyed whipped cream:

1 cup heavy whipping cream

1 cup sour cream

½ cup dark honey

Prepare an indirect medium-hot fire in your grill, with heat on one side and no heat on the other.

Lightly sprinkle the cornmeal in the bottom of a 12 x 10-inch disposable aluminum pan.

Dollop the dough down the center of the prepared pan. Drizzle lightly with olive oil and carefully spread the dough to the edges of the pan so that the dough is an even thickness throughout. Lightly make some indentations. Cover the dough evenly with the grapes, lightly pressing them down into the dough. Sprinkle with the brown sugar, a drizzle of olive oil, and the salt. Cover with plastic wrap or a damp kitchen towel and let rise a second time for about an hour.

For the honeyed whipped cream, with an electric mixer fitted with a whisk attachment, whip the cream on high speed until stiff peaks form, 6 to 7 minutes. Fold in the sour cream and honey. Set aside or keep refrigerated until ready to use.

Set the pan on the indirect side of the grill or on top of 2 or 3 bricks placed on the grill grates to elevate the focaccia and cook for about 30 minutes, until it is well browned and firm in the center, and the dough registers 190°F.

Serve warm or at room temperature, dolloped with the honeyed whipped cream.

**Y**OU CAN TURN OUR STIR-TOGETHER FLATBREAD DOUGH INTO FOCACCIA simply by brushing on a slurry of olive oil, water, and salt—which is what gives focaccia its distinctive flavor. We've added a little fresh rosemary, plus a postgrilling topping of fresh strawberries in a balsamic syrup. Make sure the balsamic is one that you like because the flavor will really come through. The flatbread bakes on the indirect side of the grill with the lid closed, so the top is what gets browned rather than the bottom. Serve this flatbread right from the cutting board for a rustic presentation.

# GRILL-BAKED FOCACCIA WITH BALSAMIC STRAWBERRIES AND FRESH ROSEMARY

SERVES 4 TO 6

**For the balsamic strawberries:**

¼ cup good balsamic vinegar

¼ cup granulated sugar

3 cups fresh strawberries, hulled and quartered

**For the focaccia:**

1 teaspoon cornmeal

2 tablespoons olive oil, plus more for the pan

1 recipe Stir-Together Flatbread Dough (page 32)

1 teaspoon fine kosher or sea salt

2 tablespoons fresh rosemary leaves

For the balsamic strawberries, combine the vinegar, sugar, and 2 tablespoons of water in a saucepan over high heat on the stovetop. Bring to a boil and stir to dissolve the sugar. Let cool. Pour over the strawberries in a medium bowl and toss to blend. Let stand for 30 minutes at room temperature, and then stir again before topping the flatbread.

For the focaccia, prepare an indirect medium-hot fire in your grill, with heat on one side and no heat on the other.

Lightly sprinkle the cornmeal in the bottom of a 12 x 10-inch disposable aluminum pan. Pat the dough into the pan. In a small bowl, combine 2 tablespoons of water with the 2 tablespoons of olive oil and the salt. Using the handle of a wooden spoon, dimple the dough but do not poke holes in it. Brush the olive oil mixture over the top of the dough so it pools in the depressions.

Place the pan on the indirect side of the grill, close the lid, and grill for 17 to 20 minutes, or until puffed, golden, and firm to the touch. Loosen the focaccia from the sides of the pan and turn out onto a cutting board, then turn right side up. Sprinkle with the rosemary and spoon the balsamic strawberries over the focaccia. Let rest for 5 minutes, then cut into pieces and serve.

# Chapter 5
## POCKETS, ROLLS, PIADINE, AND CALZONES

—◇◇◇◇◇—

Once you get the hang of making your own dough, patting or rolling it out, then grilling it, what's next? Adding a filling and trying new shapes. Again, in this chapter, we look to the Mediterranean for inspiration, including recipes traditionally prepared over an open fire with flavors from many lands.

The easiest way to start is to use ready-made pita bread, fill it, and then grill it. Store-bought pita tastes wonderful grilled with just a brush of olive oil on each side, so imagine the deliciousness of a Lebanese lamb filling and a savory compote to finish.

If you can pat or roll out a pizza or flat-bread, you can also spread on a filling, roll it all up, and cut into delightful rolls we call pizza pinwheels.

You might also want to try a piada (they are also known as *piadina*, and the plural is *piadine*), an Italian flatbread from the Romagna region. It is unleavened, and on the order of a flour tortilla. The gist is to grill it quickly on a griddle or skillet and then fold it over a filling. A piada can be a great take-away handheld "sandwich." We offer a couple of deliciously flavored doughs: the Stir-Together Piada Dough with Red Pepper and Chives (page 37) and Sun-Dried Tomato and Rosemary Piada Dough (page 38).

A grilled calzone is the ultimate handheld turnover pizza pie. And it cooks quickly, or *pronto*, as Italians would say.

We recommend using a cast-iron grill griddle or a cast-iron skillet placed directly on the grill grates for pockets, rolls, piadine, and calzones that might contain a deliciously cheesy filling that can ooze out. If you grill these on a pizza stone, the stone could absorb the oil or fat and then smoke on subsequent uses.

THIS MIDDLE EASTERN–STYLE SANDWICH IS POPULAR IN SYRIA, TURKEY, and Iran. Shawarma is the Anglicization of a Turkish word meaning "turning," as the meat for shawarma is grilled on a spit or on skewers. The lemon tahini is also delicious with grilled vegetables and fish.

# GRILLED CHICKEN SHAWARMA POCKETS WITH LEMON TAHINI

MAKES 8 PITAS

### For the lemon tahini:

1 cup tahini

1/4 cup freshly squeezed lemon juice

2 tablespoons plain yogurt

2 garlic cloves, minced

### For the shawarma pockets:

1 cup plain yogurt

1/4 cup cider vinegar

2 garlic cloves, minced

1/2 teaspoon ground cardamom

1/2 teaspoon ground allspice

Kosher salt and freshly ground black pepper

1 pound boneless chicken thighs

4 large pita breads

Extra-virgin olive oil for brushing

1/2 cucumber, thinly sliced

1 tomato, seeded and chopped

1 bunch green onions, chopped

Soak 8 (12-inch) bamboo skewers in water for at least 30 minutes.

For the lemon tahini, whisk the tahini, lemon juice, yogurt, and garlic together in a bowl. Cover and refrigerate until ready to serve.

For the shawarma pockets, whisk together the yogurt, vinegar, garlic, cardamom, and allspice to make a marinade, adjusting the seasoning to taste. Place the chicken pieces in a large resealable plastic bag and pour in the

*(recipe continues)*

marinade. Seal the bag, toss to coat, and refrigerate for at least 30 minutes or up to 8 hours, tossing occasionally.

Cut an opening for a pocket in the side of each pita bread and brush the outside with olive oil. Remove the chicken from its marinade and thread onto the 8 prepared skewers, discarding the used marinade.

Prepare a medium-hot fire in your grill.

Grill the chicken skewers for 3 to 4 minutes per side, or until the chicken is firm, opaque, and has good grill marks. Grill the pita bread on both sides until it has good grill marks. To serve, carefully slide the chicken off the skewers and into the pocket of each grilled pita. Spoon the lemon tahini inside and add cucumber, tomato, and green onion, as desired.

# TRICOLOR PEPPER SALAD WITH BASIL VINAIGRETTE

### SERVES 6

This is a perfect party salad because you make it ahead so all the flavors have time to blend. It's colorful and robust, a perfect complement to pizzas, calzones, and other grilled fare.

———— ≈ ————

1 red bell pepper

1 yellow bell pepper

1 green bell pepper

½ pound thin green beans

1 cup Kalamata olives, pitted

4 ounces feta cheese, crumbled

### For the basil vinaigrette:

¼ cup freshly squeezed lemon juice

½ cup extra-virgin olive oil

2 garlic cloves, minced

2 tablespoons chopped fresh basil

2 teaspoons granulated sugar

1 teaspoon kosher or sea salt

½ teaspoon red pepper flakes

Prepare a hot fire in your grill.

Place the peppers over the fire and turn every minute or so for about 10 minutes or more, until they are charred. Place the charred peppers in a paper sack, fold it closed, and let the peppers sit and steam for about 10 minutes. When cool, cut off the tops and remove some of the charred skin. Quarter the peppers and remove the seeds, then cut into strips and place in a large bowl.

Set a pot of salted water to boil, and prepare a large bowl of ice water. Add the green beans to the boiling water to blanch them for 3 minutes. Remove the beans from the boiling water and place them in the ice water for a couple of minutes to cool completely. Drain the cooled beans and place in the bowl with the peppers. Add the olives.

For the basil vinaigrette, in a glass jar combine the lemon juice, olive oil, garlic, basil, sugar, salt, and red pepper flakes, and shake to blend. Pour over the pepper mixture and let sit for several hours, covered, in the refrigerator. When ready to serve, spoon the vegetables onto a platter, top with the crumbled feta, and pour the dressing from the bowl over the top.

**W**E STARTED WITH A RECIPE IDEA FROM ANDRES BARRERA, CHEF AT City Winery in Chicago, and then gave this our own spin. Instead of making lamb patties, we pan-grill the loose lamb filling and spoon it into the pita pockets. The topping is a no-cook relish, perfect when plum tomatoes are plentiful at the market or from your garden.

# LEBANESE LAMB PITA POCKETS
# WITH TOMATO GINGER RELISH

MAKES 8 PITAS

### For the tomato ginger relish:

1 pound plum tomatoes, seeded and finely chopped

1/4 cup red wine vinegar

1/4 cup packed light brown sugar

1 garlic clove, minced

2 teaspoons grated fresh ginger

Kosher salt

### For the lamb pitas:

1 pound lean ground lamb

3 large garlic cloves, minced

1 small yellow or white onion, finely chopped

1 cup seeded and finely chopped tomato

1/2 cup pine nuts

3 tablespoons finely chopped fresh flat-leaf parsley

1/2 teaspoon ground allspice

1 tablespoon freshly squeezed lemon juice

1 tablespoon extra-virgin olive oil

Kosher or sea salt and freshly ground black pepper

8 large pita breads

Olive oil for brushing

4 ounces crumbled feta

Soak 8 (12-inch) bamboo skewers in water for at least 30 minutes. Prepare a medium-hot fire in your grill.

For the tomato ginger relish, stir together the tomatoes, vinegar, brown sugar, garlic, and ginger; adjust the seasoning to taste. Cover and refrigerate until ready to serve.

*(recipe continues)*

For the lamb pitas, combine the ground lamb, garlic, onion, tomatoes, pine nuts, parsley, allspice, lemon juice, olive oil, and salt and pepper in a disposable aluminum pan.

Place the pan on the grill grates, close the lid, and grill for 5 minutes. Open the lid, stir the lamb mixture, and grill for 5 more minutes with the lid down, or until the lamb is cooked through and has browned.

Cut a pocket in the side of each pita bread and brush the outside with olive oil. Grill the pita bread on both sides until it has good grill marks.

To serve, spoon the lamb filling into each grilled pita and serve with the tomato ginger relish and the crumbled feta.

J UDITH MADE THESE FOR A FAMILY GATHERING, WHERE THEY WERE devoured in minutes. The idea of a rustic, savory roll you can do on the grill adds a little fun to a backyard barbecue. To make your own Mediterranean-style flavored salt, combine 1 teaspoon of coarse kosher salt with ½ teaspoon of herbes de Provence. It is a delicious finish to sprinkle on pizzas, flatbreads, and grilled meats and vegetables.

# GOAT CHEESE, SPINACH, AND RED ONION PIZZA PINWHEELS

MAKES
12 ROLLS

1 recipe Classic Pizza Dough (or a variation, page 33) or Slow-Rise Pizza Dough (page 35)

All-purpose flour for dusting

4 ounces goat cheese, crumbled

2 cups baby spinach, larger leaves torn into smaller pieces

½ cup diced red onion

¼ cup cornmeal

Extra-virgin olive oil for brushing

1½ teaspoons Mediterranean-style salt blend (see headnote)

Place a cast-iron grill griddle on the grill grates. Prepare a medium-hot fire in your grill.

Roll out the dough to a 19 x 14-inch rectangle on a floured surface. Sprinkle the surface of the dough with the goat cheese, spinach, and onion, leaving a ½-inch border of dough. Starting with a long end, roll the dough over on itself to form a tight cylinder. Pinch the ends closed and gently squeeze the cylinder to make it uniform in width and 12 inches long. Using a serrated knife and a gentle sawing motion, slice the cylinder into 12 rolls. Place the rolls on a tray sprinkled with cornmeal. Brush the tops of the rolls generously with olive oil and sprinkle with the salt blend.

Using a grill spatula, transfer the rolls to the griddle. Close the lid and grill for 8 minutes. Check the rolls. If the underside of the rolls is getting too brown, turn them over. Close the lid and continue to grill for 8 to 12 minutes more, or until the rolls have risen and browned.

THE SAME FLAVORS THAT MAKE A BACON, LETTUCE, AND TOMATO SANDWICH taste good are even better in this rustic roll. For a vegan version, use vegan mayonnaise, then switch out the bacon for seitan or smoked tofu—or even the grilled eggplant from the Coca Escalivada (page 183). Make it your own.

# BLT PIZZA PINWHEELS

MAKES 12
ROLLS

1 recipe Classic Pizza Dough (or a variation, page 33) or Slow-Rise Pizza Dough (page 35)

All-purpose flour for dusting

2 tablespoons good-quality mayonnaise

1 garlic clove, minced

1/2 cup fresh basil leaves, larger leaves torn into smaller pieces

1/2 cup cooked and crumbled bacon

1/2 cup diced plum or cherry tomatoes

1/4 cup cornmeal

Extra-virgin olive oil for brushing

1 tablespoon coarse kosher or sea salt

Place a cast-iron grill griddle on the grill grates. Prepare a medium-hot fire in your grill.

Roll out the dough to a 19 x 14-inch rectangle on a floured surface. In a small bowl, mix the mayonnaise and garlic together. Spread this over the surface of the dough, leaving a 1/2-inch border of dough. Sprinkle with the basil, bacon, and tomatoes. Starting with a long end, roll the dough over on itself to form a tight cylinder. Pinch the ends closed and gently squeeze the cylinder to make it uniform. Using a serrated knife and a gentle sawing motion, slice the cylinder into 12 rolls. Place the rolls on a tray sprinkled with cornmeal. Brush the tops of the rolls generously with olive oil and sprinkle with the salt.

Using a grill spatula, transfer the rolls the griddle. Close the lid and grill for 8 minutes. Check the rolls. If the underside of the rolls is getting too brown, turn them over. Close the lid and continue to grill for 8 to 12 minutes more, or until the rolls have risen and browned.

# Piada Fillings

Here are some combinations that are great for piadine. Because the dough is so thin, you don't need thick slices or a lot of any of the ingredients, so the ingredients you do use need to be very flavorful. These combinations would work for panini, too.

*Mozzarella cheese, tomatoes, basil, and arugula*

*Salami, Parmesan cheese, and fresh spinach*

*Smoked salmon and boursin cheese*

*Grilled Italian sausage and peppers*

*Chicken salad and crumbled blue cheese*

*Sliced ham and fontina cheese*

*Goat cheese, sun-dried tomatoes, and mâche*

*Bacon, Brie cheese, and basil*

*Salami, Parmesan cheese, and arugula*

*Stracchino cheese and arugula*

*Mushrooms and prosciutto*

*Spinach, red onion, and fontina cheese*

*Pesto and chicken*

*Salami and creamy Parmesan dressing*

*Nutella and sliced pear (on the Basic Piada Dough, page 38)*

*Fruit preserves or jam with farmer cheese (on the Basic Piada Dough, page 38)*

EMILIA-ROMAGNA IS HOME TO SOME OF THE MOST WONDERFUL FOODS, such as pancetta, mortadella, Parmigiano-Reggiano cheese, balsamic vinegar from Modena, and much more. In this recipe we'll combine ingredients from the same terroir.

# ROASTED RED PEPPER PIADINE ROMAGNOLE

MAKES 4
PIADINE

1 recipe Stir-Together Piada Dough with Red Pepper and Chives (page 37)

All-purpose flour for dusting

1 jarred roasted red bell pepper, cut into strips

1 cup fresh baby spinach, loosely packed

4 slices prosciutto

¼ cup grated Parmigiano-Reggiano cheese

Balsamic vinegar to drizzle

Prepare a hot fire in your grill. Set a cast-iron griddle directly over the fire (or you can grill directly on the grates, if you wish).

When ready to grill, divide the dough into 4 portions. Roll them into rounds about 8 inches in diameter on a lightly floured surface. Grill them on the hot griddle or a hot fire for about 1 minute per side. The dough will bubble and brown.

Assemble each piada with one-quarter of the roasted red pepper strips, ¼ cup of spinach, a slice of proscuitto, 1 tablespoon of Parmigiano-Reggiano, and a drizzle of balsamic vinegar. Fold the piadine and eat while warm.

GROWING UP ON A LAKE, KAREN'S FAMILY CELEBRATED MEMORIAL DAY and Labor Day weekends with an outdoor Sunday breakfast on the grill. Her father would make a wood fire in the stone fireplace he built. The menu always included scrambled eggs with snipped onion chives, skillet potatoes, and bacon and sausage. Everything was extra delicious because it was cooked outdoors. This piada has all the flavors of those Sunday mornings all rolled up into one.

# RISE AND SHINE PIADINE WITH HERB SCRAMBLED EGGS AND ITALIAN SAUSAGE

MAKES 4
PIADINE

1 recipe Fresh Herb Piada Dough (page 38)

All-purpose flour for dusting

8 ounces fresh Italian sausage

4 large eggs

1 tablespoon heavy whipping cream

1 tablespoon snipped fresh chives or parsley, plus more to taste

Kosher or sea salt and freshly ground black pepper

1 tablespoon unsalted butter

Prepare a hot fire in your grill.

When ready to grill, divide the dough into 4 portions. Roll them into rounds about 8 inches in diameter on a lightly floured surface. Grill them over a hot fire or on a hot griddle for about 1 minute per side. The dough will bubble and brown. Stack, wrap in aluminum foil, and keep warm on the indirect side of the grill.

Heat a cast-iron skillet over the hot fire and cook the sausage until browned. Using a spatula, break the sausage apart into crumbles. Set off the heat, cover, keep warm, and lower the fire to medium. (If using charcoal, move the coals apart to diffuse the heat.)

Whisk together the eggs, cream, and chives with a fork and adjust the seasoning. In another cast-iron skillet, melt the butter and cook the eggs until they begin to set up or cook to your desired doneness.

Divide the scrambled eggs and sausage among the piadine. Fold over or roll each piada and eat while warm.

T HE KEY TO THIS MOST UNIVERSAL PIADA WRAP IS PAPER-THIN SLICED salami. The soppressata is similar to pepperoni, which could be substituted, as could just about any favorite salami you might like. The Asiago is a little bit softer cheese than Parmesan or Romano and melts a bit faster on this quick sandwich.

# PIADA WRAPS WITH ASIAGO AND SOPPRESSATA

MAKES 4
PIADINE

1 recipe Sun-Dried Tomato and Rosemary Piada Dough (page 38)

All-purpose flour for dusting

8 thin slices soppressata salami

½ cup shredded Asiago cheese

Extra-virgin olive oil for drizzling

Prepare a hot fire in your grill. Set a cast-iron griddle directly over the fire (or you can grill directly on the grates, if you wish).

When ready to grill, divide the dough into 4 portions. Roll them into rounds about 8 inches in diameter on a lightly floured surface. Grill them over on the hot griddle or a hot fire for about 1 minute per side. The dough will bubble and brown.

Top each piada with 2 slices of soppressata, 1 tablespoon of Asiago, and a drizzle of extra-virgin olive oil. Fold and roll each piada loosely and flatten it. Sprinkle 1 tablespoon of the remaining Asiago on the top of each piada roll. Place the piadine back on the griddle and close the lid for a minute to melt the cheese. Serve while warm.

# WATERCRESS SALAD WITH GORGONZOLA AND TOASTED WALNUTS

**SERVES 4**

This is a nice leafy salad, perfect with any kind of pizzeria offering. The balsamic dressing recipe makes more than you need for this salad but keeps refrigerated for 7 to 10 days. If you can't find watercress, substitute spinach or arugula for the cress.

≈

2 bunches watercress

1 heart romaine lettuce

½ cup Gorgonzola cheese

½ cup walnuts, toasted

**For the balsamic dressing:**

½ cup vegetable oil

3 tablespoons balsamic vinegar

1 garlic clove, minced

½ teaspoon kosher or sea salt

Rinse and dry the watercress and romaine. Remove and discard the woody stems from the cress and place it in a bowl. Chop the romaine into ½-inch strips and add to the bowl.

For the balsamic dressing, in a glass jar, combine the oil, vinegar, garlic, and salt and shake to blend. Pour about 4 tablespoons of the dressing over the greens and toss to coat. Arrange on a platter and top with the crumbled Gorgonzola and toasted walnuts. Serve the remaining dressing on the side.

WE LIKE THE SLOW-RISE PIZZA DOUGH (PAGE 35) BEST OF ALL FOR THE calzones, but the Classic Pizza Dough (page 33) works very well, too, and is ready in an hour. Calzones are half-moon-shaped turnover pizzas whose dough edges are crimped to hold together. They are cheesy and gooey, typically filled with ricotta, mozzarella, Parmesan, or provolone cheese.

# GRILLED CALZONES WITH ITALIAN SAUSAGE, ARTICHOKE, AND RICOTTA

MAKES 4
CALZONES

1 recipe Slow-Rise Pizza Dough (page 35) using either variation: Garlic and Herb Pizza Dough or Whole Wheat Pizza Dough (Page 33 to 34)

All-purpose flour for dusting

1 cup cooked and crumbled fresh Italian sausage

½ cup ricotta cheese

¼ cup grated Pecorino Romano cheese

¼ cup grated fontina cheese

⅓ cup artichoke hearts (jarred or canned)

3 tablespoons chopped sun-dried tomatoes

Zest of 1 lemon

2 tablespoons freshly squeezed lemon juice

Prepare a medium-hot fire in your grill.

When ready to grill, divide the dough into 4 portions. Roll them into rounds about 6 inches in diameter on a lightly floured surface.

In a food processor or a bowl, combine the sausage, ricotta, Romano, fontina, artichoke hearts, sun-dried tomatoes, lemon zest, and lemon juice. Pulse to combine. The mixture should be chunky. Spoon equal amounts of the mixture into the center of each circle of dough, spreading to within 1 inch of the edge. Fold over each circle of the dough to form a half-moon. Crimp the dough edges to seal in the stuffing. Place the calzones directly on the grill grates or on a hot griddle and grill for about 3 minutes per side, until nicely browned. Serve at once.

PANZEROTTI ARE SMALLER VERSIONS OF CALZONES, MADE WITH A SOFTER dough such as our pizza doughs in this book. They are perfect for a late-afternoon appetizer, with a glass of Chianti or pinot grigio.

# THREE-CHEESE SPINACH PANZEROTTI

**MAKES 6 PANZEROTTI**

1 teaspoon extra-virgin olive oil

1½ cups spinach leaves

2 garlic cloves, minced

⅓ cup ricotta cheese

⅓ cup grated mozzarella cheese

⅓ cup grated Parmesan cheese

Kosher or sea salt and freshly ground black pepper

1 recipe Slow-Rise Pizza Dough (page 35) using either variation: Garlic and Herb Pizza Dough or Whole Wheat Pizza Dough (Page 33 to 34)

All-purpose flour, for dusting

½ cup San Marzano Pizza Sauce (page 177) or store-bought pizza sauce

In a skillet, heat the oil and add the spinach, tossing and cooking until just wilted, about 2 minutes. Add the garlic and cook for another 2 minutes. Let cool.

In a bowl, combine the cooled spinach mixture with the cheeses and stir to blend. Adjust the seasoning to taste.

Prepare a medium-hot fire in your grill.

When ready to grill, divide the dough into 6 portions. Roll them into rounds about 4 inches in diameter on a lightly floured surface.

Spoon equal amounts of the spinach mixture into the center of each circle of dough, spreading to within 1 inch of the edge. Drizzle 1½ tablespoons of the pizza sauce over the spinach mixture on each calzone. Fold over each circle of dough to form a half-moon. Crimp the dough edges to seal in the stuffing.

Place the panzerotti directly on the grill grates or on a hot griddle and grill for about 3 minutes per side, until nicely browned. Serve at once.

# MEMPHIS-STYLE COLESLAW WITH 1-MINUTE VINAIGRETTE

Pulled pork sandwiches topped with vinegar-dressed coleslaw are a staple in the South, especially in Memphis. Serve this alongside the BBQ Pulled Pork Calzones (page 138). The dressing makes more than you need to dress the slaw, but it keeps for a couple of weeks in the refrigerator and is perfect for any green salad or use it for the Sautéed Corn and Wilted Lettuce Salad (page 195).

1 (10-ounce) bag shredded coleslaw mix

**For the 1-minute vinaigrette:**

½ cup vegetable oil

½ cup white vinegar

1 garlic clove, minced

1 teaspoon salt

4 teaspoons granulated sugar

Pinch of red pepper flakes

Place the coleslaw in a large bowl.

For the 1-minute vinaigrette, in a glass jar, combine the vegetable oil, vinegar, garlic, salt, sugar, and red pepper flakes. Shake to blend. Pour ⅓ to ½ cup of the dressing over the coleslaw. Toss to blend and serve at once.

HERE IS OUR AMERICAN VERSION OF CALZONES, WITH A FILLING OF SPICY pulled pork. You can buy pulled pork, slow-smoke it, or even cook it in a slow cooker. We use just a bit of Parmesan cheese in each of the calzones, even though you might not normally think of pairing cheese and barbecue.

# BBQ PULLED PORK CALZONES

MAKES 4
CALZONES

1 recipe Slow-Rise Pizza Dough (page 35) or Classic Pizza Dough (page 33)

All-purpose flour for dusting

1½ cups shredded pulled pork

⅓ cup spicy barbecue sauce, such as Sweet Baby Ray's

½ cup Parmesan cheese

Prepare a medium-hot fire in your grill.

When ready to grill, divide the dough into 4 portions. Roll them into rounds about 6 inches in diameter on a lightly floured surface.

Combine the pulled pork and barbecue sauce and spoon equal amounts of the pork mixture into the center of each circle of dough, spreading to within 1 inch of the edge. Sprinkle each calzone with 2 tablespoons of the Parmesan. Fold over each circle of dough to form a half-moon. Crimp the dough edges to seal in the stuffing.

Grill them over a hot fire or on a hot griddle for about 3 minutes per side, until nicely browned. Serve at once.

# Chapter 6

## PIZZA ON THE GRILL GRATES

Grilling pizza dough directly on the grill grates gives you more caramelized grill flavor than does grilling on a pizza stone, but you'll have to be ready to "flip out." The technique behind these pizzas involves a sturdy dough, parchment paper, a light rather than a heavy topping, and an indirect fire. The pizzas are 6- to 8-inch rounds that can also be referred to as *pizzettes*, which simply means "small pizzas."

Sturdier doughs, from the Slow-Rise Pizza Dough (page 35) and Classic Pizza Dough (page 33) to the Garlic and Herb Pizza Dough (page 33), Whole Wheat Pizza Dough (page 34), and Herbed Gluten-Free Pizza Dough (page 36), hold the circular shape better than the more freeform Stir-Together Flatbread Dough does. However, if you would rather shape your pizza into an oblong, oval, or square, or leave it free-form, please do so.

After preparing the dough, line a baking sheet with parchment paper and oil the top of the parchment. Place a pizza round on the oiled parchment and brush the top of the pizza round with olive oil. When you're at the grill, simply pick up the parchment and flip the unadorned pizza circle onto the hot grill grates, quickly peeling off the parch-ment in one deft movement. Placing the dough on the parchment paper first and then flipping it upside down on the grill grates helps keep the dough's shape better than if you tried to place the dough directly on the grill grates by hand. This quick flip-and-peel motion is easy once you do it a time or two. Keeping the pizzas small also makes them easier to maneuver on the grill.

When you are removing the parchment paper during the flip, the underside of the pizza will get little ridges, sort of like a waffle. This helps any sauce or toppings hold to the pizza better. After the big flip, return the used parchment to the baking sheet, oil it, and get another pizza dough round ready. You can use the same piece of parchment paper over and over for all the pizzas in the recipe, as long as you remem-ber to re-oil it before placing the next piece of dough on it.

Grill each pizza on one side until it has grill marks, then turn the pizza and transfer it to the indirect side with grill tongs. (The grill marks help you lift the pizza easily with tongs.) Once the pizza is on the indirect side of the grill, add toppings that don't require much cooking. Closing the grill lid lets the cheese and toppings melt together.

SOME MIGHT CALL THIS A KID'S PIZZA, WITH SUCH SIMPLE INGREDIENTS. But when the homemade dough blisters over a charcoal fire, this basic grilled cheese pizza is fit for a Neapolitan! You can choose to sauce or keep it as a white pizza. Or better yet, prepare half of the pizzettes with sauce and half of them without.

# SUBLIME CHEESE PIZZA

**MAKES 4
(6- TO 8-INCH) PIZZAS**

1 recipe Classic Pizza Dough (page 33) or Herbed Gluten-Free Pizza Dough (page 36)

All-purpose flour for rolling out and dusting

⅔ cup shredded fontina cheese

⅔ cup shredded robiola cheese

⅔ cup shredded buffalo mozzarella cheese

Extra-virgin olive oil for brushing

½ cup San Marzano Pizza Sauce (page 177) (optional)

6 to 8 tablespoons chopped fresh basil, or more to taste

Divide the dough into 4 portions. On a floured surface, pat or roll each portion into a 6- to 8-inch-diameter circle.

Prepare an indirect medium-hot fire in your grill, with heat on one side and no heat on the other.

In a large bowl, combine the 3 cheeses and toss to blend.

Line a baking sheet with parchment paper. Brush olive oil into a circle that's a little larger than your pizza, and then place your pizza on the oiled circle. Brush the top of the pizza with olive oil.

Lift the pizza by holding the ends of the parchment paper. At a height of about 6 inches above the grill, flip the circle of dough onto the hot side of the grill grates. Quickly peel off the parchment and close the lid. Grill the pizza for 2 to 3 minutes, or until it has good grill marks. Turn the pizza with tongs and move it to the indirect side. Spoon on 2 tablespoons of the pizza sauce, if you like. Top with ¼ cup of the cheese mixture. Cover and grill for 2 to 3 minutes, or until the cheese has melted. Repeat the process with the other pizzas. Top the pizzettes with the shredded basil. Serve hot.

ADDING CHIVES TO THIS PESTO MAKES IT A BRILLIANT GREEN, JUST LIKE the green color in the Italian flag. Plus it makes for a smooth and creamy pesto. Make it ahead of time when basil and chives are in season. Label and store in your freezer for up to 6 months. You can use store-bought pesto, if you prefer.

# MOZZARELLA AND CHIVE-BASIL PESTO PIZZA

**MAKES 4 (6- TO 8-INCH) PIZZAS**

### For the chive-basil pesto:

1 cup roughly chopped onion or garlic chives

1 cup packed fresh basil leaves

¼ cup walnut halves or pieces, toasted

1 garlic clove, minced

¾ cup olive oil

½ cup freshly grated Parmesan or Romano cheese

Kosher or sea salt and freshly ground black pepper

### For the pizza:

1 recipe Classic Pizza Dough (page 33) or Slow-Rise Pizza Dough (page 35)

All-purpose flour for rolling out and dusting

Extra-virgin olive oil for brushing

4 ounces fresh mozzarella cheese, thinly sliced

Prepare an indirect medium-hot fire in your grill, with heat on one side and no heat on the other.

For the chive-basil pesto, in a food processor, process the chives, basil, walnuts, and garlic to a fine paste. Slowly add the olive oil in a steady stream until the pesto is creamy and then add the cheese and pulse again. Adjust the seasonings to taste.

Divide the dough into 4 portions. On a floured surface, pat or roll each portion into a 6- to 8-inch-diameter circle.

*(recipe continues)*

Line a baking sheet with parchment paper. Brush olive oil into a circle that's a little larger than your pizza, and then place your pizza on the oiled circle. Brush the top of the pizza with olive oil.

Lift the pizza by holding the ends of the parchment paper. At a height of about 6 inches above the grill, flip the circle of dough onto the hot side of the grill grates. Quickly peel off the parchment and close the lid. Grill the pizza for 2 to 3 minutes, or until it has good grill marks. Turn the pizza with tongs and move it to the indirect side. Spoon 2 to 3 tablespoons of pesto onto the pizza and spread to cover, leaving a 1/2-inch border. Top with one-quarter of the mozzarella. Cover and grill for 2 to 3 minutes, or until the cheese has melted. Repeat the process with the other pizzas and serve.

# Best Melting Cheeses

When you think pizza, chances are, you think mozzarella. It's the default pizza cheese, and understandably so. It melts well, has a mild flavor that goes with almost any pizza toppings, and blends well with other cheeses. It's stretchy and stringy and holds its place on a pizza. It's also easy to find and affordable. But a world of other cheeses is out there. So here is a cheat sheet to expand your stash of cheeses and your pizza repertoire.

### *Stretchy and stringy melting cheeses that stay in place on a pizza or in a panino:*

| | | |
|---|---|---|
| Mozzarella | Queso Oaxaca | Swiss |
| Provolone | Scamorza | |

### *Smooth melters, ranging from flowing cheeses to those that soften gently and hold some shape:*

| | | |
|---|---|---|
| Asiago | Cheddar | Gruyère |
| Brie (the rind does not melt) | Chihuahua | Havarti |
| Burrata | Emmentaler | Monterey Jack |
| Camembert (the rind does not melt) | Fontina | Muenster |
| | Gorgonzola | Raclette |
| | Gouda | Roquefort |

### *Slower-melting cheeses that hold their shape do well combined with other ingredients, used in a sauce, or sprinkled on top:*

| | | |
|---|---|---|
| Aged Asiago | Goat cheese | Romano |
| Feta | Parmesan | |
| Gruyère | Ricotta | |

CLAMS AND OTHER FRESH SHELLFISH NEED HIGHER HEAT TO OPEN ON the grill, so grill those first. Once they're done, you can grill the pizzettes, then put them together for a "Why didn't I think of that before?" feast. Mussels would also work for this pizza. The rule of thumb for grilling shellfish is this: If a clam or mussel is open before grilling or stays closed after grilling, discard it.

# CLAM PIZZETTES WITH GARLIC, CHILE, AND OREGANO OIL

**MAKES 4 (6- TO 8-INCH) PIZZAS**

### For the garlic, chile, and oregano oil:

2 garlic cloves, minced

½ teaspoon dried red pepper flakes

1 teaspoon dried oregano

¼ teaspoon salt

½ cup extra-virgin olive oil

### For the clam pizzettes:

4 pounds tightly closed fresh littleneck or Manila clams, scrubbed and debearded

1 recipe Garlic and Herb Pizza Dough (page 33) or Herbed Gluten-Free Pizza Dough (page 36)

All-purpose flour for rolling out and dusting

¼ cup grated Pecorino Romano cheese

For the garlic, chile, and oregano oil, stir together the garlic, red pepper flakes, oregano, salt, and olive oil in a small bowl. Set aside.

For the clam pizzettes, prepare an indirect medium-hot fire in your grill, with heat on one side and no heat on the other.

Arrange the clams on a perforated grill rack or in a large disposable aluminum pan directly over the fire. Close the lid and grill for 3 to 4 minutes. Open and stir the clams. Remove any that have opened. Close the lid and grill for 3 to 4 minutes more. Remove the clams that have opened and discard those that have not. Place all the opened clams in a large serving bowl or on a deep platter.

Divide the dough into 4 portions. On a floured surface, pat or roll each portion into a 6- to 8-inch-diameter circle.

Line a baking sheet with parchment paper. Brush olive oil into a circle that's a little larger than your pizza, and then place your pizza on the oiled circle. Brush the top of the pizza with the garlic, chile, and oregano oil.

*(recipe continues)*

Lift the pizza by holding the ends of the parchment paper. At a height of about 6 inches above the grill, flip the circle of dough onto the hot side of the grill grates. Quickly peel off the parchment and close the lid. Grill the pizza for 2 to 3 minutes, or until it has good grill marks. Turn the pizza with tongs and move it to the indirect side. Brush the pizza with more garlic, chile, and oregano oil and sprinkle with one-quarter of the cheese. Cover and grill for 2 to 3 minutes, or until the cheese has melted. Repeat the process with the other pizzas. To serve, scoop the clams from their shells to top each pizza.

FEATURING FRESH VEGETABLES FROM YOUR GARDEN (OR LEFTOVER grilled vegetables), this pizza provides a vegetarian entrée that's colorful with big flavor. Additional condiments to serve alongside this pizza include the Parmesan Aïoli (page 57), Kalamata Olive Paste (page 104), and Chive-Basil Pesto (page 144).

# SUMMER GARDEN PIZZA

**MAKES 4
(6- TO 8-INCH) PIZZAS**

1 recipe Classic Pizza Dough (page 33) or Herbed Gluten-Free Pizza Dough (page 36)

All-purpose flour for rolling out and dusting

Extra-virgin olive oil for brushing

¼ cup finely chopped yellow summer squash

¼ cup finely chopped zucchini

¼ cup finely chopped red onion

¼ cup chopped cherry tomatoes

½ cup freshly grated Parmesan cheese

Snipped fresh herbs, such as flat-leaf parsley, basil, chives, and oregano

Prepare an indirect medium-hot fire in your grill, with heat on one side and no heat on the other.

Divide the dough into 4 portions. On a floured surface, pat or roll each portion into a 6- to 8-inch-diameter circle.

Line a baking sheet with parchment paper. Brush olive oil into a circle that's a little larger than your pizza, and then place your pizza on the oiled circle. Brush the top of the pizza with olive oil.

Lift the pizza by holding the ends of the parchment paper. At a height of about 6 inches above the grill, flip the circle of dough onto the hot side of the grill grates. Quickly peel off the parchment and close the lid. Grill the pizza for 2 to 3 minutes, or until it has good grill marks. Turn the pizza with tongs and move it to the indirect side. Sprinkle the pizza with one-quarter of all the toppings. Cover and grill for 2 to 3 minutes, or until the cheese has melted. Repeat the process with the other pizzas.

T O EVERY SEASON (TURN, TURN, TURN), THERE IS A PIZZA, AND THIS ONE belongs to spring. Gather the season's freshest baby leeks, spring onions, shallots, and chives. No need for chopping; just strew the long strands of grilled onions atop each pizza. If you want to make this vegan, skip the cheese. It has plenty of flavor without it.

# SPRING ONION PIZZA

**MAKES 4
(6- TO 8-INCH) PIZZAS**

6 baby or 3 medium-size leeks

1 bunch green or spring onions, trimmed and rinsed

1 recipe Classic Pizza Dough (or a variation, page 33) or Herbed Gluten-Free Pizza Dough (page 36)

All-purpose flour for rolling out and dusting

Extra-virgin olive oil for brushing

2 shallots, diced

4 ounces goat cheese, crumbled

¼ cup snipped fresh chives (and chive blossoms, if you have them)

Prepare an indirect medium-hot fire in your grill, with heat on one side and no heat on the other.

Cut off and discard the root ends of the leeks and slice them in half lengthwise. Swish the leeks in cold water to remove the dirt and pat dry. Brush the leeks and green onions with olive oil.

Place the leeks and green onions perpendicular to the grill grates (or on a perforated grill rack). Grill until the green onions are blistered, 3 to 4 minutes, and the leeks are crisp-tender, turning often, 8 to 10 minutes.

Divide the dough into 4 portions. On a floured surface, pat or roll each portion into a 6- to 8-inch-diameter circle.

Line a baking sheet with parchment paper. Brush olive oil into a circle that's a little larger than your pizza, and then place your pizza on the oiled circle. Brush the top of the pizza with olive oil.

Lift the pizza by holding the ends of the parchment paper. At a height of about 6 inches above the grill, flip the circle of dough onto the hot side of the grill grates. Quickly peel off the parchment and close the lid. Grill the pizza for 2 to 3 minutes, or until you have good grill marks.

*(recipe continues)*

Turn the pizza with tongs and move it to the indirect side. Sprinkle with the shallots and top with one-quarter of the grilled leeks, green onions, and goat cheese. Cover and grill for 2 to 3 minutes, or until the cheese has melted. Repeat the process with the other pizzas. To serve, sprinkle with chives.

Salad on the Side

# GRILLED ASPARAGUS SALAD

**SERVES 4**

While you've got the grill going, why not do the salad, too?

———— ≋ ————

1 pound asparagus, trimmed

Olive oil for brushing

Kosher or sea salt and freshly ground black pepper

**For the classic vinaigrette:**

3 tablespoons extra-virgin olive oil

1 tablespoon freshly squeezed lemon juice

½ teaspoon Dijon mustard

1 garlic clove, minced

Parmesan cheese for shaving, as needed

Snipped fresh herbs, such as flat-leaf parsley, basil, chives, and lemon balm

Prepare a medium-hot fire in your grill.

Place the asparagus on a baking sheet, drizzle with olive oil, and season with salt and pepper.

Grill the asparagus directly over the fire, perpendicular to the grill grates, for 3 to 4 minutes per side, turning often, or until crisp-tender. Arrange the asparagus on a platter.

For the classic vinaigrette, place the olive oil, lemon juice, mustard, and garlic in a glass jar with a tight-fitting lid. Shake to blend. Pour the vinaigrette over the asparagus. Use a vegetable peeler to shave the Parmesan, to your liking, over the asparagus and sprinkle with fresh herbs. Serve warm or at room temperature.

**I**N THE BAY AREA, PIZZA LOVERS GO WILD FOR SPRING NETTLES AND BABY arugula on pizza. While nettles can be difficult to find (and prickly to pick), arugula has become more widely available. So just imagine you're at Chez Panisse in Berkeley, Pizzaiolo in Oakland, or Flour + Water in San Francisco. You can, of course, do these same toppings with Brick Oven–Style Dough (page 34), in the brick oven style (page 22), to be even more authentic.

# BABY ARUGULA, RICOTTA, SEA SALT, AND OLIVE OIL PIZZETTES

MAKES 4
(6- TO 8-INCH) PIZZAS

1 cup ricotta cheese

¼ teaspoon dried red pepper flakes

2 tablespoons extra-virgin olive oil

¼ teaspoon coarse sea salt

Freshly ground black pepper

1 recipe Garlic and Herb Pizza Dough (page 33), Slow-Rise Pizza Dough (page 35), or Herbed Gluten-Free Pizza Dough (page 36)

All-purpose flour for rolling out and dusting

Extra-virgin olive oil for brushing

¼ cup grated Pecorino Romano cheese

4 cups baby arugula (about 6 ounces)

Stir together the ricotta, red pepper flakes, and olive oil in a small bowl and adjust the seasonings to taste. Set aside.

Prepare an indirect medium-hot fire in your grill, with heat on one side and no heat on the other.

Divide the dough into 4 portions. On a floured surface, pat or roll each portion into a 6- to 8-inch-diameter circle.

Line a baking sheet with parchment paper. Brush olive oil into a circle that's a little larger than your pizza, and then place your pizza on the oiled circle. Brush the top of the pizza with olive oil.

Lift the pizza by holding the ends of the parchment paper. At a height of about 6 inches above the grill, flip the circle of dough onto the hot side of the grill grates. Quickly peel off the parchment and close the lid. Grill the pizza for 2 to 3 minutes, or until it has good grill marks. Turn the pizza with tongs and move it to the indirect side. Spread the pizza with one-quarter of the ricotta mixture and sprinkle with one-quarter of the Pecorino Romano. Cover and grill for 2 to 3 minutes, or until the cheese has melted. Repeat the process with the other pizzas. To serve, top each pizza with 1 cup of arugula.

WITH A COLD BEER ON A HOT NIGHT, THIS PIZZA PROVIDES ALL THE fireworks your taste buds will require. Green curry paste, available in the Asian section of the grocery store, contains green chiles, lemongrass, and other tasty seasonings. There'll be plenty of shrimp, so you can nibble on some of them and put the rest on the pizzettes.

# THAI SHRIMP PIZZETTES WITH COCONUT AND CHILES

MAKES 4
(6- TO 8-INCH) PIZZAS

**For the green curry coconut sauce:**

1 cup canned coconut milk, well shaken

2 teaspoons green curry paste

Juice of 1 lime (about 1 tablespoon)

**For the shrimp pizzettes:**

1 pound large shrimp (31–35 count), peeled and deveined

Extra-virgin olive oil for brushing

1 recipe Classic Pizza Dough (page 33), Slow-Rise Pizza Dough (page 35), or Herbed Gluten-Free Pizza Dough (page 36)

All-purpose flour for rolling out and dusting

¼ cup chopped fresh cilantro

For the green curry coconut sauce, stir together the coconut milk, green curry paste, and lime juice in a small bowl. Set aside.

For the shrimp pizzettes, soak 8 (12-inch) bamboo skewers in water for at least 30 minutes.

Prepare an indirect medium-hot fire in your grill, with heat on one side and no heat on the other.

Thread the shrimp onto the prepared skewers and brush with olive oil.

Grill the shrimp over direct heat for 3 to 4 minutes per side, or until firm, opaque, and pink.

Divide the dough into 4 portions. On a floured surface, pat or roll each portion into a 6- to 8-inch-diameter circle.

Line a baking sheet with parchment paper. Brush olive oil into a circle that's a little larger than your pizza, and then place your pizza on the oiled circle. Brush the top of the pizza with olive oil.

Lift the pizza by holding the ends of the parchment paper. At a height of about 6 inches above the grill, flip

*(recipe continues)*

the circle of dough onto the hot side of the grill grates. Quickly peel off the parchment and close the lid. Grill the pizza for 2 to 3 minutes, or until it has good grill marks. Turn the pizza with tongs and move it to the indirect side. Spread the pizza with one-quarter of the green curry coconut sauce. Cover and grill for 2 to 3 minutes, or until the topping has melted. Repeat the process with the other pizzas. To serve, top each pizza with grilled shrimp and cilantro.

**T**HIS IS OUR GRILLED VERSION OF THE FAMOUS SMOKED SALMON AND caviar pizza that Wolfgang Puck created in 1982 and still serves to the A-list stars on Oscars night. The cold salmon and caviar are a perfect contrast to the crispy hot pizza crust. Be prepared to spend a pretty penny on the Osetra caviar—or substitute a less expensive black roe instead.

# OSCAR-WORTHY SMOKED SALMON PIZZETTES

**MAKES 4 (6- TO 8-INCH) PIZZAS**

1 recipe Classic Pizza Dough (page 33), Slow-Rise Pizza Dough (page 35), or Herbed Gluten-Free Pizza Dough (page 36)

All-purpose flour for rolling out and dusting

Extra-virgin olive oil for brushing

1 cup sour cream

2 tablespoons chopped fresh dill

Freshly ground black pepper

1 red onion, slivered

1 lemon, halved

16 ounces smoked salmon, cut into paper-thin slices

¼ cup salmon caviar

¼ cup black Osetra caviar

4 teaspoons snipped fresh chives

Prepare an indirect medium-hot fire in your grill, with heat on one side and no heat on the other.

Divide the dough into 4 portions. On a floured surface, pat or roll each portion into a 6- to 8-inch-diameter circle.

Line a baking sheet with parchment paper. Brush olive oil into a circle that's a little larger than your pizza, and then place your pizza on the oiled circle. Brush the top of the pizza with olive oil.

In a small bowl, combine the sour cream, dill, and a grind or two of pepper.

Lift the pizza by holding the ends of the parchment paper. At a height of about 6 inches above the grill, flip the circle of dough onto the hot side of the grill grates. Quickly peel off the parchment and close the lid. Grill the pizza for 2 to 3 minutes, or until it has good grill marks. Turn the pizza with tongs and move it to the indirect side. Spread the pizza with one-quarter of the sour cream mixture and sprinkle with one-quarter of the red onion slivers. Cover and grill for 2 to 3 minutes to warm through. Repeat

*(recipe continues)*

the process with the other pizzas. At the same time, place the lemon halves directly over the fire and grill for 3 or 4 minutes, until they are browned and hot. To serve, top each pizza with one-quarter of the salmon, 1 tablespoon of each of the caviars, a squeeze of grilled lemon juice, and a sprinkle of chives.

# MEDITERRANEAN ORANGE SALAD
## WITH TOASTED PECANS AND GOAT CHEESE

### SERVES 4

Use blood oranges or tangerines and their zest when they are in season. Serve this sharp salad with a rich pizza.

---

**For the orange zest dressing:**

Grated zest of 1 large orange

⅓ cup white wine vinegar

⅔ cup vegetable oil

2 garlic cloves

1 teaspoon kosher or sea salt

4 teaspoons granulated sugar

**For the salad:**

1 head red leaf lettuce, torn into bite-size pieces

2 oranges, peeled, pith removed, and segmented

16 Kalamata olives, pitted

4 ounces goat cheese, crumbled

¼ cup chopped pecans or hazelnuts, toasted

For the orange zest dressing, combine all of the ingredients in a glass jar with a tight-fitting lid. Shake to blend. It will keep in the refrigerator for several days.

For the salad, arrange the lettuce on 4 salad plates. Place one-quarter of the orange segments and four of the olives on each plate. Crumble the goat cheese on top of each salad. Drizzle with the dressing and sprinkle with the nuts. Serve immediately.

INSTEAD OF SERVING A REGULAR SALAD WITH BREAD AND BUTTER, SERVE A mini-pizzette topped with chicken Caesar salad. It's the salad and bread all rolled into one. You can grill the chicken breast yourself or visit the grocery store and scoop up a cup from the salad bar. This makes more dressing than you'll need, but it keeps refrigerated for 5 to 7 days.

# HANDHELD GRILLED CHICKEN
# CAESAR MINI PIZZETTES

**MAKES 8 (3- TO 4-INCH)
MINI PIZZAS**

### For the Caesar salad dressing:

½ cup extra-virgin olive oil

2 tablespoons grated Romano or Parmesan cheese

2 tablespoons mayonnaise

2 tablespoons freshly squeezed lemon juice

1 tablespoon Dijon mustard

1 teaspoon anchovy paste

1 garlic clove, minced

Kosher or sea salt

4 cups chopped romaine lettuce

1 cup chopped grilled chicken

### For the mini pizzettes:

1 recipe Classic Pizza Dough (page 33), Slow-Rise Pizza Dough (page 35), or Herbed Gluten-Free Pizza Dough (page 36)

All-purpose flour for rolling out and dusting

Olive oil for brushing

Freshly ground black pepper

Freshly shaved Parmesan cheese for the topping

Prepare an indirect medium-hot fire in your grill, with heat on one side and no heat on the other.

In a bowl, combine the olive oil, cheese, mayonnaise, lemon juice, mustard, anchovy paste, and garlic, and season with salt to taste. Mix together with a handheld immersion blender. In a larger bowl, combine the lettuce and chicken and dress with about 4 tablespoons of the dressing. Set aside.

For the mini pizzettes, divide the dough into 8 portions. On a floured surface, pat or roll each portion into a 3- to 4-inch-diameter circle.

Line a baking sheet with parchment paper. Prepare 2 of these mini pizzettes at a time. Brush olive oil into 2 circles a little larger than each pizza, and then place each dough round on an oiled circle. Brush the top of the rounds with olive oil.

Lift the dough by holding the ends of the parchment paper. At a height of about 6 inches above the grill, flip the circles of dough onto the hot side of the grill grates. Quickly peel off the parchment and close the lid. Grill the pizzettes for 2 to 3 minutes, or until they have good grill marks. Turn the pizzettes with tongs and move them to the indirect side. Cover and grill for 1 to 2 minutes, until lightly browned. Repeat the process with the other pizzettes. To serve, top each pizzette with the Caesar salad mixture, freshly ground pepper, and several shavings of Parmesan.

**T**HIS DELICIOUS COMBINATION IS COLORFUL AS WELL AS TASTY. THE topping can also be served over pasta or rice and is a surprisingly good pizza.

# STIR-GRILLED SALMON, SUGAR SNAP PEAS, **AND** TEARDROP TOMATO PIZZA

8 ounces salmon steak
or fillets, cubed

4 ounces sugar snap peas
or snow peas, strings
removed

12 cherry tomatoes, halved

½ red onion, sliced
into slivers

Extra-virgin olive oil
for brushing

Kosher or sea salt and freshly
ground black pepper

1 recipe Classic Pizza
Dough (page 33), Garlic and
Herb Pizza Dough (page 33),
or Whole Wheat Pizza
Dough (page 34)

All-purpose flour
for rolling out and dusting

½ cup grated Romano or
Parmesan cheese

Prepare an indirect medium-hot fire in your grill, with heat on one side and no heat on the other.

In an oiled grill wok or grill basket set on top of a baking sheet, combine the salmon, sugar snap peas, tomatoes, and onion. Drizzle lightly with olive oil and season with salt and pepper. Set the basket above the fire. Stir-grill for 6 to 8 minutes, until the salmon is opaque, using 2 long-handled wooden spoons to toss the mixture. Move the wok to the indirect side of the grill. Close the lid on the grill and cook for another 3 to 4 minutes, to finish cooking the salmon. Set aside.

Divide the dough into 4 portions. On a floured surface, pat or roll each portion into a 6- to 8-inch-diameter circle.

Line a baking sheet with parchment paper. Brush olive oil into a circle that's a little larger than your pizza, and then place your pizza on the oiled circle. Brush the top of the pizza with olive oil.

Lift the pizza by holding the ends of the parchment paper. At a height of about 6 inches above the grill, flip the circle of dough onto the hot side of the grill grates. Quickly peel off the parchment and close the lid. Grill the pizza for 2 to 3 minutes, or until it has good grill marks. Turn the pizza with tongs and move it to the indirect side. Spread the pizza with one-quarter of the stir-grilled mixture and 2 tablespoons of the cheese. Cover and grill for 2 to 3 minutes. Repeat the process with the other pizzas. Serve hot.

S O MANY VARIETIES OF REALLY GREAT CHICKEN AND TURKEY SAUSAGE are available nowadays. When Whole Foods Market opened in Kansas City, the sausage display case, with about 20 different offerings, meant grilling sausage was no humdrum affair anymore. Choose any kind of artisan sausage for this recipe. Grill up more than you need for this pizza. In fact, make double the caramelized red onions, too. Left-over artisan sausage, red onions, and Brie can be made into a delectable panini for you the next day (see chapter 3).

# CHICKEN SAUSAGE AND CARAMELIZED RED ONION PIZZA

MAKES 4 (6- TO 8-INCH) PIZZAS

Extra-virgin olive oil for brushing

2 pounds red onion, thinly sliced

1 tablespoon chopped fresh thyme

1/4 cup white wine

3 links fresh chicken sausage

1 recipe Classic Pizza Dough (page 33) or Whole Wheat Pizza Dough (page 34)

All-purpose flour for rolling out and dusting

1 apple, cored and thinly sliced

4 ounces Brie cheese, thinly sliced

Prepare an indirect medium-hot fire in your grill, with heat on one side and no heat on the other.

Over medium-high heat on the stovetop, in a large skillet coated with olive oil, sweat the onion, covered. Stir periodically so that the onions do not stick and burn on the bottom of the pan. After 20 minutes, remove the lid and add the thyme and white wine. Continue to cook for an additional 20 minutes, until the onion is well caramelized. The onion should cook down by about half in volume. The caramelized onion can be cooked 2 or 3 days in advance and refrigerated until ready to use. It can also be frozen for several months.

At the same time, grill the chicken sausages over high heat for 6 to 8 minutes, turning them to brown all sides. Set the browned sausages in the indirect side of the grill for another 10 to 12 minutes with the grill lid closed to finish cooking the sausages.

Slice the grilled chicken sausages ¼ inch thick on the diagonal.

Divide the dough into 4 portions. On a floured surface, pat or roll each portion into a 6- to 8-inch-diameter circle.

Line a baking sheet with parchment paper. Brush olive oil into a circle that's a little larger than your pizza, and then place your pizza on the oiled circle. Brush the top of the pizza with olive oil.

Lift the pizza by holding the ends of the parchment paper. At a height of about 6 inches above the grill, flip the circle of dough onto the hot side of the grill grates. Quickly peel off the parchment and close the lid. Grill the pizza for 2 to 3 minutes, or until it has good grill marks. Turn the pizza with tongs and move it to the indirect side. Spread the pizza with one-quarter of the caramelized onions and sausage, and arrange the slices of apples and Brie like wagon wheel spokes. Cover and grill for 2 to 3 minutes. Repeat the process with the other pizzas. Serve hot.

# Chapter 7

# PIZZA ON
# THE PIZZA STONE

Grilling pizza dough on a pizza stone has distinct advantages. You can make bigger pizzas, use less olive oil, and get a crisper crust. It won't have the charry flavor of pizza on the grill grates or the high-heat brick oven–style pizza, but it will still have the flavor of the grill. The technique behind these pizzas involves a pizza stone, grill griddle, cast-iron skillet, or other material that will hold the grill's heat and grill-bake the pizza. You want to make sure the pizza stone is on the grill as soon as you build the fire, so it has time to heat up along with the grill. You also want to make sure that you use a thick pizza stone specifically meant for the grill; the grill's higher heat can cause a thin stone or baking stone meant for the oven to crack. Heat the stone with the grill lid closed so more of the heat stays inside the grill.

You'll also need a flexible cutting board or pizza peel sprinkled with cornmeal, grill tongs, and a medium-hot fire.

Sturdier doughs, from the Classic Pizza Dough (page 33) to the Garlic and Herb Pizza Dough (page 33), Whole Wheat Pizza Dough (page 34), and Herbed Gluten-Free Pizza Dough (page 36), hold the circle shape better than the more free-form Stir-Together Flatbread Dough does.

After preparing the dough and creating medium-size pizza rounds (take care to roll out the dough to no larger than your cutting board or pizza peel and the baking stone you're using; you don't want the dough to flop off the sides), transfer each pizza round to a cornmeal-dusted flexible cutting board or pizza peel. The cornmeal acts like little ball bearings to help slide the dough off the peel and onto the pizza stone—just make sure you don't let the pizza sit for longer than a few minutes on the cornmeal. The cornmeal can absorb the liquid from the dough and then not do its job.

When you're at the grill, simply pick up the peel with an unadorned pizza on it, and hold it in front of the pizza stone. With a quick jerk or back-and-forth movement, slide the dough circle off the peel and onto the hot stone. Once you do this a time or two, it will be easy.

Close the lid and let one side grill-bake. Then open the lid, use grill tongs or a grill spatula to turn the pizza over, add your toppings, close the lid, and finish grill-baking.

TIP: *If you want to practice in advance, simply slide a formed pizza from the cornmeal-dusted peel onto your kitchen counter. You'll get the feel of the movement that way.*

THIS SPANISH PIZZA FROM ANDALUCIA IS SIMPLICITY ITSELF. USE IBERICO or Serrano ham and shaved Manchego cheese for an authentic flavor. Manchego has a flavor similar to aged pecorino, so this is the Spanish equivalent of the Tuscan prosciutto and pecorino duo. Enjoy this with a small glass of chilled fino or dry sherry for a tapas experience in your own backyard.

# COCA ANDALUCIA

**MAKES 2
(12-INCH) PIZZAS**

1 recipe Classic Pizza Dough (page 33) or Herbed Gluten-Free Pizza Dough (page 36)

All-purpose flour for rolling and dusting

¼ cup cornmeal for sprinkling

Extra-virgin olive oil for brushing

8 ounces thinly sliced Serrano or Iberico ham

8 ounces shaved Manchego cheese

Prepare a medium-hot fire in your grill with a pizza stone on the grill grates. Close the grill lid.

Divide the dough into 2 portions. On a floured surface, pat or roll each portion into a 12-inch-diameter circle.

Sprinkle a pizza peel or a flexible cutting board with half of the cornmeal. Arrange a pizza circle on the cornmeal-dusted peel.

Hold the pizza peel level with the grill rack so that the dough round will slide onto the center of the hot pizza stone. With a quick forward jerk of your arm, slide the dough round from the peel to the stone. Close the lid and let grill-bake for 2 to 4 minutes, or until the crust is browned on the bottom and firm. Turn the pizza crust with tongs and brush quickly with olive oil. Dot with half of the ham and cheese. Cover and grill for 2 to 3 minutes, or until the cheese has melted. Repeat the process with the other pizza.

I F YOU PLAN AHEAD, YOU CAN TRY THIS WITH THE SLOW-RISE PIZZA DOUGH (page 35), which needs 24 hours to rise. Slow-Rise Pizza Dough has a slight sourdough flavor and a wonderful "bite." With really good pepperoni, fresh mushrooms, pizza sauce, and two cheeses, this classic combination tastes even better on the grill. The kiss of smoke comes from dry wood chips smoldering on or near the fire.

# CLASSIC PEPPERONI AND MUSHROOM PIZZA WITH A KISS OF SMOKE

MAKES 2
(12-INCH) PIZZAS

⅔ cup shredded fontina or provolone cheese

⅔ cup shredded buffalo mozzarella cheese

1 recipe Classic Pizza Dough (page 33), Herbed Gluten-Free Pizza Dough (page 36), or Slow-Rise Pizza Dough (page 35)

All-purpose flour for rolling and dusting

¼ cup cornmeal for sprinkling

½ cup San Marzano Pizza Sauce (page 177)

½ cup sliced pepperoni

1 cup thinly sliced fresh mushrooms

Prepare a medium-hot fire in your grill with a pizza stone on the grill grates over direct heat.

In a large bowl, combine the cheeses and toss to blend.

If you're using a gas grill, place 1 cup of dry wood chips, such as hickory, mesquite, or apple wood chips in an aluminum foil packet with holes poked in it or a metal smoker box next to or near the pizza stone. If you're using a charcoal grill, sprinkle the chips through the grill grates onto the embers below. Close the grill lid. When you see the first wisp of smoke, the grill is ready.

Divide the dough into 2 portions. On a floured surface, pat or roll each portion into a 12-inch-diameter circle.

Sprinkle a pizza peel or a flexible cutting board with half of the cornmeal. Arrange a pizza circle on the cornmeal-dusted peel.

Hold the pizza peel level with the grill rack so that the dough round will slide onto the center of the hot pizza stone. With a quick forward jerk of your arm, slide the dough round from the peel to the stone. Close the lid and

*(recipe continues)*

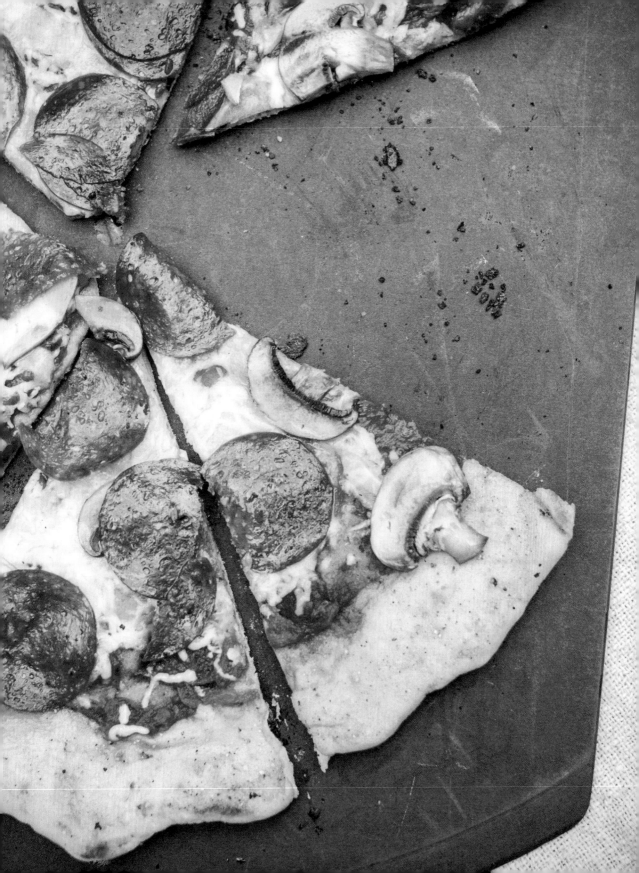

grill-bake for 2 to 4 minutes, or until the crust is browned on the bottom and firm. Turn the pizza crust with tongs and spread quickly with half of the pizza sauce. Dot with half of the pepperoni and mushrooms, and sprinkle with half of the cheese. Cover and grill for 2 to 3 minutes, or until the cheese has melted. Repeat the process with the other pizza.

# SAN MARZANO PIZZA SAUCE

Often the simplest of ingredients are the best and that is the case with our San Marzano Tomato Sauce. You can buy store-bought pizza sauce in a jar or a can, but why, when this is so simple to make. You may substitute whole tomatoes for the crushed or chopped; they'll just take longer to break down into a sauce.

1 (28-ounce) can San Marzano tomatoes, crushed or chopped

1 tablespoon extra-virgin olive oil

1 tablespoon unsalted butter

2 garlic cloves, minced

4 whole basil leaves

½ teaspoon kosher salt, or more to taste

Place all the ingredients in a saucepan and bring to a boil on the stovetop. Stir, cover, and lower the heat. Simmer for 30 minutes. Spoon the sauce over a pizza crust or pasta.

THIS VEGAN SPANISH "PIZZA," KNOWN AS A COCA, COMES FROM CATALONIA and Mallorca. Traditionally, this flatbread is baked in communal wood-burning ovens, and it can also be done in the brick oven style (page 11). A coca can be a meal in itself, a snack, or part of a tapas offering—great for entertaining. You can get the same wood-burning-oven flavor by using fine wood chips in your grill.

# COCA CATALONIA
# WITH A KISS OF SMOKE

MAKES 2
(12-INCH) PIZZAS

2 garlic cloves, minced

2 teaspoons coarse kosher or sea salt

6 tablespoons extra-virgin olive oil

2 tablespoons freshly squeezed lemon juice

1 recipe Classic Pizza Dough (page 33), Herbed Gluten-Free Pizza Dough (page 36), or Slow-Rise Pizza Dough (page 35)

All-purpose flour for rolling and dusting

¼ cup cornmeal for sprinkling

2 cups seeded and diced tomatoes

2 small zucchini, sliced paper thin

¼ cup pine nuts

16 pitted oil-cured black olives

In a small bowl, combine the garlic, salt, olive oil, and lemon juice.

Prepare a medium-hot fire in your grill with a pizza stone on the grill grates over direct heat.

If you're using a gas grill, place 1 cup of dry wood chips, such as oak, in an aluminum foil packet with holes poked in it or a metal smoker box next to or near the pizza stone. If you're using a charcoal grill, sprinkle the chips through the grill grates onto the embers below. Close the grill lid. When you see the first wisp of smoke, the grill is ready.

Divide the dough into 2 portions. On a floured surface, pat or roll each portion into a 12-inch-diameter circle.

Sprinkle a pizza peel or a flexible cutting board with half of the cornmeal. Arrange a pizza circle on the cornmeal-dusted peel.

Hold the pizza peel level with the grill rack so that the dough round will slide onto the center of the hot pizza stone. With a quick forward jerk of your arm, slide the dough round from the peel to the stone. Close the lid and let grill-bake for 2 to 4 minutes, or until the crust is browned on the bottom and firm. Turn the pizza crust with tongs and spread quickly with half of the garlic oil. Dot with half of the tomatoes and zucchini, and sprinkle with half of the pine nuts and olives. Cover and grill for 2 to 3 minutes, or until the vegetables have sizzled. Repeat the process with the other pizza.

FOR A WEEKNIGHT MEAL OR A WEEKEND BRUNCH, THIS PIZZA TASTES delicious with a glass of bubbly or a Mimosa. Bitter curly salad greens feature in this deconstructed French bistro dish that usually includes bacon lardons and a poached egg; our egg gets cooked on the grill. If you can't find frisée, try curly endive or escarole. You use these greens to outline a little nest for the egg on each pizza, so the egg stays in the center. Because of the olive oil drizzle, we suggest you make this on a nonporous ceramic pizza stone, two cast-iron skillets, or a cast-iron grill griddle.

# FRISÉE, LARDON, AND EGG PIZZA ON THE PLANCHA

**MAKES 4 (6- TO 8-INCH) PIZZAS**

1 recipe Classic Pizza Dough (page 33) or Herbed Gluten-Free Pizza Dough (page 36)

All-purpose flour for rolling out and dusting

8 ounces frisée, curly endive, or escarole, torn into small pieces

2 tablespoons extra-virgin olive oil, plus more for brushing and drizzling

¼ cup cornmeal for sprinkling

½ cup chopped green onions

8 ounces bacon lardons or chopped pancetta, cooked until crisp

4 large eggs

Kosher or sea salt and freshly ground black pepper

Prepare a medium-hot fire in your grill with a large cast-iron grill griddle on the grill grates. Close the grill lid.

Divide the dough into 4 portions. On a floured surface, pat or roll each portion into a 6- to 8-inch-diameter circle.

Toss the greens with 2 tablespoons of olive oil in a bowl until they glisten.

Sprinkle a pizza peel or a flexible cutting board with half of the cornmeal. Arrange a pizza circle on the cornmeal-dusted peel.

*(recipe continues)*

Hold the pizza peel level with the grill rack so that the dough round will slide onto the center of the hot grill griddle. With a quick forward jerk of your arm, slide the dough round from the peel to the stone. Quickly slide a second pizza circle onto the grill griddle. Close the lid and let grill-bake for 2 to 4 minutes, or until the crust is browned on the bottom and firm. Turn the pizza crusts with tongs and brush quickly with olive oil. Dot with half of the green onion and bacon lardoons, Create a circle of frisée in the center of each pizza. Crack an egg onto each pizza. Drizzle the egg with olive oil. Cover and grill for 2 to 4 minutes, or until the egg is cooked to your liking. Adjust the seasoning to taste. Repeat the process with the other pizzas.

E SCALIVADA, A SPANISH SPREAD MADE FROM GRILLED EGGPLANT AND red bell pepper, is a natural for this vegan pizza on the grill. Grill the eggplant and peppers, then put the pizza stone on the grill, go inside to prepare the escalivada, and when you come back outside, the pizza stone will be ready to go.

# COCA ESCALIVADA

**MAKES 2
(12-INCH) PIZZAS**

1 small eggplant, ends trimmed, cut into 1-inch-thick lengthwise slices

3 tablespoons extra-virgin olive oil plus more for brushing

1 red bell pepper

6 garlic cloves, minced

1 teaspoon smoked paprika

1 teaspoon ground coriander

1 teaspoon ground cumin

1 tablespoon sherry vinegar, or more to taste

Kosher salt and freshly ground pepper

1 recipe Garlic and Herb Pizza Dough (page 33) or Herbed Gluten-Free Pizza Dough (page 36)

All-purpose flour for rolling and dusting

¼ cup cornmeal for sprinkling

Prepare a medium-hot fire in your grill, with a pizza stone on one side of the grill.

Brush the eggplant slices with olive oil. Place the eggplant slices and the whole red bell pepper on the grill grates. Grill the eggplant for 4 to 5 minutes per side, turning once, until the eggplant has softened and has good grill marks. Grill the red pepper, turning every 5 minutes or so, until it has blistered all over. When the vegetables are cool enough to handle, roughly chop the eggplant. Core, seed, and skin the red bell pepper, then chop roughly. Transfer the vegetables to a medium bowl.

Heat the 3 tablespoons olive oil in a small saucepan on the stovetop and sauté the garlic over medium-high heat until golden and softened, about 3 minutes. Stir in the smoked paprika. Pour the garlic mixture over the vegetables in the bowl. Add the coriander, cumin, and sherry vinegar. Mash with a fork or a potato masher until well blended. Adjust the seasoning to taste.

Divide the dough into 2 portions. On a floured surface, pat or roll each portion into a 12-inch-diameter circle.

*(recipe continues)*

Sprinkle a pizza peel or a flexible cutting board with half of the cornmeal. Arrange a pizza circle on the cornmeal-dusted peel.

Hold the pizza peel level with the grill rack so that the dough round will slide onto the center of the hot pizza stone. With a quick forward jerk of your arm, slide the dough round from the peel to the stone. Close the lid and let grill-bake for 2 to 4 minutes, or until the crust is browned on the bottom and firm. Turn the pizza crust with tongs and spread quickly with half of the escalivada. Cover and grill for 2 to 3 minutes, or until the escalivada is warm to the touch. Repeat the process with the other pizza.

# GRILLED ANTIPASTO VEGETABLE PLATTER

**SERVES 6**

Shop in your garden or at the farmers' market and pick some fresh vegetables, slice them and brush with olive oil, grill them quickly, then arrange them on a platter in a row with like vegetables. The mortar-and-pestle dressing is done in seconds and this small amount—surprisingly—dresses a large platter of vegetables. Instead of goat cheese, try crumbles of blue cheese, queso fresco, or feta. This makes lots, but is oh so good. Consider using some of the dressed veggies for your pizza topping, too.

≈

## For the mortar-and-pestle dressing:

1 large garlic clove

1 teaspoon coarse kosher or sea salt

3 tablespoons extra-virgin olive oil

1 tablespoon freshly squeezed lemon juice

## For the grilled vegetables:

Olive oil for drizzling

2 small zucchini, ends trimmed, cut lengthwise into ½-inch-thick slices

2 small yellow summer squash, ends trimmed, cut lengthwise into ½-inch-thick slices

2 small eggplants, ends trimmed, cut lengthwise into ½-inch-thick slices

2 red onions, trimmed, peeled, and cut into ½-inch-thick slices

1 medium-size red bell pepper

1 medium-size yellow or orange bell pepper

Fine kosher or sea salt and freshly ground black pepper

1 cup brine-cured Kalamata or niçoise olives, pitted

6 ounces goat cheese or other crumbled cheese

*(recipe continues)*

For the mortar-and-pestle dressing, place the garlic and salt in a mortar and crush with the pestle. Keep crushing in a circular motion until the garlic is a smooth paste. Stir in the olive oil and lemon juice with the pestle and adjust the seasoning to taste. Set aside.

Prepare a hot fire in your grill.

Drizzle a baking sheet with olive oil and set the zucchini, squash, eggplant, onion slices, and whole bell peppers on it. Quickly turn the vegetable slices in the oil to coat them, then roast, seasoning them with salt and pepper.

Grill the slices, turning once, for 3 to 4 minutes per side, or until they have good grill marks. You may need to grill the eggplant a little longer, until it is soft and flexible. Grill the bell peppers, turning several times, until the skins are charred and blistered all over. Set the grilled vegetables back on the baking sheet.

Let the bell peppers cool slightly, then remove the skins, seeds, and stems with a paring knife and discard; slice into strips. Arrange all the vegetables on a platter. Spoon the dressing over all and top with the olives and crumbled goat cheese. Serve at room temperature.

THIS PIZZA IS FOR AVID TOMATO LOVERS, WHETHER YOU GROW THE tomatoes yourself or shop the farmers' market for interesting varieties, such as Brandywine, Cherokee Purple, Chocolate Cherry, Green Zebra, or Golden Jubilee. The idea is to have a wonderful assortment of colorful tomato slices on your pizza drizzled with the piquant white French salad dressing. You'll have leftover dressing and extra tomato slices for a side platter.

# GRILL-ROASTED TOMATO PIZZA ALLA PLANCHA

**MAKES 4
(6- TO 8-INCH) PIZZAS**

### For the white French salad dressing:

½ yellow onion, cut into 4 pieces

1 garlic clove, minced

1 tablespoon freshly squeezed lime juice

2 teaspoons tarragon vinegar

¼ teaspoon salt

¼ teaspoon freshly ground white pepper

1 cup mayonnaise

### For the tomato pizzas:

1 recipe Classic Pizza Dough (page 33) or Herbed Gluten-Free Pizza Dough (page 36)

All-purpose flour for rolling and dusting

2 pounds tomatoes, assorted varieties and colors (see headnote)

¼ cup cornmeal for sprinkling

Olive oil for brushing

Kosher or sea salt and freshly ground black pepper

4 tablespoons chopped fresh herbs, such as chives or basil

For the white French salad dressing, in a food processor, combine the onion, garlic, lime juice, and tarragon vinegar. Pulse several times to purée the onion and garlic. Add the salt, white pepper, and mayonnaise and pulse to blend. Transfer to a container and refrigerate until using.

Prepare a medium-hot fire in your grill with a cast-iron grill griddle on the grill grates. Close the grill lid.

For the tomato pizzas, divide the dough into 4 portions. On a floured surface, pat or roll each portion into 6- to 8-inch-diameter circle.

Slice each tomato 1/8 inch thick and set on the baking sheet, keeping like colors together.

Sprinkle a pizza peel or a flexible cutting board with half of the cornmeal. Arrange a pizza circle on the cornmeal-dusted peel.

Hold the pizza peel level with the grill rack so that the dough round will slide onto the center of the hot grill griddle. With a quick forward jerk of your arm, slide the dough round from the peel to the stone. Quickly slide a second pizza circle onto the grill griddle. Close the lid and grill-bake for 2 to 4 minutes, or until the crust is browned on the bottom and firm. Turn the pizza crusts with tongs and brush quickly with olive oil. Arrange a thin overlapping layer of tomatoes onto the crust, alternating the colors and sizes. Cover and grill for 2 to 4 minutes. Season lightly with salt and pepper, and top with a healthy drizzle of the dressing and a sprinkle of herbs. Repeat the process with the other pizzas.

**K**AREN REMEMBERS BUYING THE MOST BEAUTIFUL SALAD IN A BAG AT A small farmers' market in Hanalei on the north side of Kauai. It was filled with a mixture of fresh mesclun greens and flowers. The idea of sprinkling edible flowers on a pizza seems just right for this one. The sweet pineapple contrasts with the peppery tang of the nasturtiums and the mellow saltiness of the prosciutto.

# GRILLED PINEAPPLE AND PROSCIUTTO PIZZA WITH NASTURTIUMS

MAKES 2
(12-INCH) PIZZAS

8 (¼- to ⅜-inch-thick) slices fresh pineapple

1 recipe Brick Oven–Style Dough (page 34), Slow-Rise Pizza Dough (page 35), or Herbed Gluten-Free Pizza Dough (page 36)

All-purpose flour for rolling and dusting

¼ cup cornmeal for sprinkling

¼ cup Parmesan or Romano cheese

8 paper-thin slices prosciutto

10 nasturtium flowers

Prepare a medium-hot fire in your grill with a pizza stone on the grill grates over direct heat.

Grill the pineapple slices for about 2 minutes on each side, until they have good grill marks.

Divide the dough into 2 portions. On a floured surface, pat or roll each portion into a 12-inch-diameter circle.

Sprinkle a pizza peel or a flexible cutting board with half of the cornmeal. Arrange a pizza circle on the cornmeal-dusted peel.

Hold the pizza peel level with the grill rack so that the dough round will slide onto the center of the hot pizza stone. With a quick forward jerk of your arm, slide the dough round from the peel to the stone. Close the lid and grill-bake for 2 to 4 minutes, or until the crust is browned on the bottom and firm. Turn the pizza crust with tongs and sprinkle quickly with half of the cheese. Place half of the prosciutto slices on the pizza, then place 1 pineapple ring in the middle of the pizza and the other 3 rings around it. Cover and grill for 2 to 3 minutes. Repeat the process with the other pizza. Then scatter half of the nasturtiums on each pizza and serve.

**W**E LOVE THIS ROASTED RED PEPPER SAUCE FOR ITS FULL FLAVOR AND ease of preparation. Make it a couple of days ahead of time. It will keep refrigerated for 5 to 7 days.

# ITALIAN SAUSAGE AND ONION PIZZA WITH ROASTED RED PEPPER SAUCE

**MAKES 2 (12-INCH) PIZZAS**

**For the roasted red pepper sauce:**

**4 roasted red peppers (jarred ones work fine)**

**½ red onion, quartered**

**1 garlic clove, minced**

**2 teaspoons balsamic vinegar**

**Kosher or sea salt and freshly ground black pepper**

**1 recipe Brick Oven–Style Dough (page 34), Slow-Rise Pizza Dough (page 35), or Herbed Gluten-Free Pizza Dough (page 36)**

**All-purpose flour for rolling and dusting**

**¼ cup cornmeal for sprinkling**

**½ cup grated Romano cheese**

**½ red onion, slivered**

**1 pound fresh Italian sausage, cooked and crumbled**

Prepare a medium-hot fire in your grill with a pizza stone on the grill grates over direct heat.

For the roasted red pepper sauce, in a food processor, combine the red peppers, onion, garlic, and vinegar, and purée. Adjust the seasoning to taste. Set aside.

Divide the dough into 2 portions. On a floured surface, pat or roll each portion into a 12-inch-diameter circle.

Sprinkle a pizza peel or a flexible cutting board with half of the cornmeal. Arrange a pizza circle on the cornmeal-dusted peel.

Hold the pizza peel level with the grill rack so that the dough round will slide onto the center of the hot pizza stone. With a quick forward jerk of your arm, slide the dough round from the peel to the stone. Close the lid and grill-bake for 2 to 4 minutes, or until the crust is browned on the bottom and firm. Turn the pizza crust with tongs and spread quickly with half of the red pepper sauce. Sprinkle with half of the Romano cheese, half of the red onion slivers, and half of the cooked Italian sausage. Cover and grill for 2 to 3 minutes, or until the cheese has melted. Repeat the process with the other pizza.

THIS IS A WONDER OF A PIZZA AND PERFECT FOR USING UP SUMMER SQUASH at its peak growing season. The squash is sliced thinly so it is easier to layer on the pizza. Don't turn the squash slices: You'll get great grill marks on one side. Arrange them on the pizzas, grill marks–up.

# GRILLED SUMMER SQUASH AND GOAT CHEESE PIZZA

MAKES 2
(12-INCH) PIZZAS

**For the lemony goat cheese–olive spread:**

8 ounces soft goat cheese, at room temperature

½ cup pitted and finely chopped Kalamata olives

2 tablespoons finely chopped onion

1 teaspoon grated lemon zest

1 tablespoon freshly squeezed lemon juice

1 to 2 tablespoons olive oil (optional)

2 small zucchini, ends trimmed, cut lengthwise into ⅛-inch-thick slices

2 small yellow summer squash, ends trimmed, cut lengthwise into ⅛-inch-thick slices

Extra-virgin olive oil for drizzling

1 recipe Brick Oven–Style Dough (page 34), Slow-Rise Pizza Dough (page 35), or Herbed Gluten-Free Pizza Dough (page 36)

All-purpose flour for rolling and dusting

¼ cup cornmeal for sprinkling

Prepare a medium-hot fire in your grill with a pizza stone on the grill grates over direct heat.

For the lemony goat cheese–olive spread, in a medium bowl, combine the goat cheese, olives, onion, lemon zest, and lemon juice. Stir to blend. If the mixture is thick, add 1 to 2 tablespoons of olive oil to thin it.

Place the squash in a large bowl and drizzle with oil. Toss the squash to lightly coat in oil, and grill on one side only for 2 or 3 minutes, until it has good grill marks. Set aside.

*(recipe continues)*

Divide the dough into 2 portions. On a floured surface, pat or roll each portion into a 12-inch-diameter circle.

Sprinkle a pizza peel or a flexible cutting board with half of the cornmeal. Arrange a pizza circle on the cornmeal-dusted peel.

Hold the pizza peel level with the grill rack so that the dough round will slide onto the center of the hot pizza stone. With a quick forward jerk of your arm, slide the dough round from the peel to the stone. Close the lid and grill-bake for 2 to 4 minutes, or until the crust is browned on the bottom and firm. Turn the pizza crust with tongs and spread quickly with half of the goat cheese mixture. Arrange the squash strips like wagon wheel-spokes, alternating the colors. Cover and grill for 2 to 3 minutes. Repeat the process with the other pizza.

*Salad on the Side*

# SAUTÉED CORN AND WILTED LETTUCE SALAD

**SERVES 6**

Summertime means fresh vegetables and this simple salad makes the most of two farmers' market standouts: corn and tomatoes. Try this salad as a topper for potato, pepper, and onion pizzas.

───────≈───────

6 cups tender salad greens

2 Roma tomatoes, seeded and diced

⅓ cup 1-Minute Vinaigrette (page 137) or store-bought Italian dressing

2 ears fresh sweet corn, kernels cut from the cob

Place the salad greens and diced tomatoes in a large bowl.

In a small skillet over medium-high heat on the stovetop, cook the vinaigrette and corn kernels together for 3 to 4 minutes. The corn will sputter and pop a bit.

Pour the mixture over the salad greens, toss well, and serve immediately, just as the greens are starting to wilt.

**C**APRESE ALMOST RHYMES WITH "EASY," AND THAT IS EXACTLY TRUE OF this brilliant summer salad that we are putting on top of a pizza.

# CLASSIC CAPRESE

SERVES 2 OR 3

1 recipe Garlic and Herb
Pizza Dough (page 33),
Slow-Rise Pizza Dough
(page 35), or Herbed Gluten-
Free Pizza Dough (page 36)

All-purpose flour
for rolling and dusting

¼ cup cornmeal
for sprinkling

Olive oil for brushing

12 (¼-inch-thick) slices
beefsteak tomato

12 (¼-inch-thick) slices
buffalo mozzarella

Kosher or sea salt
to taste and freshly
ground black pepper

12 fresh basil leaves, torn

Prepare a medium-hot fire in your grill with a pizza stone on the grill grates over direct heat.

Divide the dough into 2 portions. On a floured surface, pat or roll each portion into a 12-inch-diameter circle.

Sprinkle a pizza peel or a flexible cutting board with half of the cornmeal. Arrange a pizza circle on the cornmeal-dusted peel.

Hold the pizza peel level with the grill rack so that the dough round will slide onto the center of the hot pizza stone. With a quick forward jerk of your arm, slide the dough round from the peel to the stone. Close the lid and grill-bake for 2 to 4 minutes, or until the crust is browned on the bottom and firm. Turn the pizza crust with tongs and brush quickly with olive oil. Alternate half of the tomato and mozzarella slices in concentric circles, with 4 slices each of the tomatoes and mozzarella toward the edge of the pizza and 2 slices of each in the center. Cover and grill for 2 to 3 minutes, or until the cheese has softened and begun to melt. Scatter half of the torn basil leaves on top of the pizza and serve. Repeat the process with the other pizza.

THIS IS A TAKE ON ONE OF THE MOST POPULAR DIPS OF RECENT TIME. IT'S perfect alone or with additions of grilled red pepper strips, Italian sausage, pepperoni, chicken, mushrooms, or prosciutto—or a combination. It's also a great spread for a grilled chicken or turkey panini or for slathering on bruschetta.

# SPINACH ARTICHOKE PIZZA
## WITH WOOD SMOKE

MAKES 2
(12-INCH) PIZZAS

### For the spinach-artichoke dip:

½ cup mayonnaise

½ cup sour cream

½ cup shredded mozzarella cheese

½ cup grated Parmesan or Romano cheese

1 cup chopped artichoke hearts (jarred or canned)

2 cups packed chopped fresh spinach

1 tablespoon freshly squeezed lemon juice

### For the pizza:

1 recipe Classic Pizza Dough (page 33), Herbed Gluten-Free Pizza Dough (page 36), or Slow-Rise Pizza Dough (page 35)

All-purpose flour for rolling and dusting

¼ cup cornmeal for sprinkling

For the spinach-artichoke dip, in a large bowl, combine the mayonnaise, sour cream, cheeses, artichoke hearts, spinach, and lemon juice and toss to blend.

Prepare a medium-hot fire in your grill with a pizza stone on the grill grates over direct heat.

If you're using a gas grill, place 1 cup of dry wood chips, such as hickory, mesquite, or apple, in an aluminum foil packet with holes poked in it or a metal smoker box next to or near the pizza stone. If you're using a charcoal grill, sprinkle the chips through the grill grates onto the embers below. Close the grill lid.

When you see the first wisp of smoke, the grill is ready.

Divide the dough into 2 portions. On a floured surface, pat or roll each portion into a 12-inch-diameter circle.

Sprinkle a pizza peel or a flexible cutting board with half of the cornmeal. Arrange a pizza circle on the cornmeal-dusted peel.

Hold the pizza peel level with the grill rack so that the dough round will slide onto the center of the hot pizza stone. With a quick forward jerk of your arm, slide the dough round from the peel to the stone. Close the lid and grill-bake for 2 to 4 minutes, or until the crust is browned on the bottom and firm. Turn the pizza crust with tongs and spread quickly with half of the spinach-artichoke dip. Cover and grill for 2 to 3 minutes, or until the mixture bubbles and browns. Repeat the process with the other pizza.

# Chapter 8
# BRICK OVEN–STYLE PIZZA

If you want authentic Neapolitan-style pizza with characteristic *cornicione* (charry spots on the crust), your grill can deliver. Although Neapolitan brick, stone, or ceramic ovens bake pizzas at 900°F for only 60 to 90 seconds, that's a little too hot and fast for most grills. At temperatures of 650° to 700°F degrees—which are well within your reach on the grill—your pizza will cook in 2 to 3 minutes and still have the cornicione and delicious flavor of the brick oven.

Many grill manufacturers now market pizza inserts for both charcoal and gas grills (see page 14). You can also create a pizza insert yourself. Using two pizza stones and firebricks from your barbecue shop or hardware store, you can make an open-ended, box-shaped oven that you can place right on the grill grates. You use the firebricks for the three walls and the pizza stones for the base and roof. You want your pizza insert to be just tall enough to slide a pizza in and out. The general idea of these pizza inserts is to create a brick-oven effect in which high heat is captured and concentrated around the pizza, not dispersed throughout the grill. Depending on the type of grill you have, the pizza insert may also need to fit under the grill lid as you preheat the grill and the pizza oven insert.

You'll also need a flexible dough that can be rolled very thinly, a metal pizza peel sprinkled with cornmeal, and a hot fire. The dough has to be thin enough that it can cook in a short time.

Our dough of choice is Brick Oven–Style Pizza Dough (page 34), made with Italian "00" flour that is ground so fine it's like baby powder. Look for Caputo, Aria, or Delverde brands of "doppio zero" or "00" flour at Italian markets or online. Just remember to roll out the dough to no larger than the pizza peel and pizza stone you're using. You don't want the dough to flop off the sides.

After preparing the dough and shaping the dough rounds, transfer each pizza round to a cornmeal-dusted flexible pizza peel. Quickly add the toppings to the pizza on the peel.

When you're at the grill, simply pick up the peel loaded with the pizza, and hold it in front of the pizza oven insert. With a quick jerk or back-and-forth movement, slide the dough circle off the peel and onto the hot stone in the pizza oven. Once you do this a time or two, it will be easy.

To remove the pizza from the pizza oven, use your peel or the combination of grill tongs and peel. Transfer it to a cutting board and serve.

TIP: *If you want to practice in advance, simply slide the formed pizza from the cornmeal-dusted peel onto your kitchen counter. You'll get the feel of the movement that way.*

THE CLASSIC TOMATO, MOZZARELLA, AND BASIL PIZZA GETS A LITTLE spoonful of cream drizzled in the center as it comes out of the pizza oven. The cream adds the final note of deliciousness.

# NEAPOLITAN MARGHERITA PIZZA

**MAKES 2
(12-INCH) PIZZAS**

1 recipe Brick Oven–Style Dough (page 34)

All-purpose flour
for rolling and dusting

¼ cup cornmeal
for sprinkling

Extra-virgin olive oil for brushing

½ cup San Marzano Pizza Sauce (page 177)

16 fresh basil leaves

8 ounces sliced buffalo mozzarella or fior di latte or whole-milk mozzarella cheese

2 tablespoons heavy whipping cream

Preheat the grill and the pizza oven insert on high heat until the temperature reaches 650° to 700°F.

Divide the dough into 2 portions. Hand toss, or, on a floured surface, pat or roll each portion into a 12-inch-diameter circle.

Sprinkle a pizza peel or a flexible cutting board with half of the cornmeal. Arrange a pizza circle on the cornmeal-dusted peel. Brush with olive oil. Spread with half of the pizza sauce, leaving a ½-inch border. Then arrange the basil and cheese on top.

Hold the pizza peel level with the grill rack so that the pizza will slide onto the center of the hot pizza stone. With a quick forward jerk of your arm, slide the pizza from the peel to the stone. Grill for 2 to 3 minutes, or until the cheese has melted. Slide the peel under the pizza and remove it from the pizza oven. Spoon half of the cream in the center of the pizza and serve hot. Repeat the process with the other pizza.

Salad on the Side

# ITALIAN FENNEL SALAD

## MAKES 4 SERVINGS

This is a refreshingly crisp salad that pairs well with bruschetta, panini, and pizza.

———— ≈ ————

1 medium-size fennel bulb, trimmed (keep some of the feathery fronds for garnish)

4 ounces Parmesan cheese, very thinly sliced

8 ounces button mushrooms, thinly sliced

¼ cup extra-virgin olive oil

1 to 2 tablespoons freshly squeezed lemon juice

Kosher or sea salt and freshly ground black pepper

Slice the fennel bulb thinly from the top to the base. Lay out the slices on a serving plate and top with the Parmesan and mushroom slices. Drizzle with the olive oil and lemon juice, adjust the seasoning to taste, and serve at room temperature.

THIS IS JUDITH'S FAVORITE THAT SHE ALWAYS ORDERS AT SPIN! NEAPOLITAN Pizza in the Kansas City area. Thin slices of potato get crispy brown, joined by the flavors of pancetta, green onion, roasted red pepper, and goat cheese. With a good salad and a glass of red wine, that's amore.

# POTATO, PANCETTA, GREEN ONION, AND GOAT CHEESE PIZZA

**MAKES 2 (12-INCH) PIZZAS**

8 new potatoes, boiled until just fork-tender

2 tablespoons extra-virgin olive oil, plus more for brushing and drizzling

1 recipe Brick Oven–Style Dough (page 34)

All-purpose flour for rolling and dusting

¼ cup cornmeal for sprinkling

½ cup diced pancetta, cooked until crisp

½ cup finely chopped green onion

½ cup finely chopped roasted red pepper

8 ounces goat cheese crumbled

Preheat the grill and the pizza oven insert on high heat until the temperature reaches 650° to 700°F.

Thinly slice the boiled potatoes and place in a bowl. Gently toss the potato slices with the 2 tablespoons of olive oil.

Divide the dough into 2 portions. Hand toss, or, on a floured surface, pat or roll each portion into a 12-inch-diameter circle.

Sprinkle a pizza peel or a flexible cutting board with half of the cornmeal. Arrange a pizza circle on the corn-meal-dusted peel. Brush with olive oil. Spread with half of the potato slices, leaving a ½-inch border. Then, arrange half of the pancetta, green onion, roasted red pepper, and goat cheese on top.

Hold the pizza peel level with the grill rack so that the pizza will slide onto the center of the hot pizza stone. With a quick forward jerk of your arm, slide the pizza from the peel to the stone. Grill for 2 to 3 minutes, or until the cheese has melted and the potato slices have browned on the edges. Slide the peel under the pizza and remove it from the pizza oven. Repeat the process with the other pizza.

INSPIRED BY A SIMILAR PIZZA AT PIZZERIA MOZZA IN LOS ANGELES, THIS ONE is a salute to summer. Pick your own squash blossoms from your zucchini and yellow summer squash plants, find them at farmer's markets, or use very thinly sliced baby zucchini instead. Burrata is a toothsome cheese made from mozzarella and cream. It's a smooth pillow of mozzarella with a creamy, soft center.

# SQUASH BLOSSOM, TOMATO, AND BURRATA PIZZA

**MAKES 2 (12-INCH) PIZZAS**

8 large squash blossoms, rinsed, and patted dry, or 4 baby zucchini, thinly sliced lengthwise

1 tablespoon extra-virgin olive oil, plus more for brushing and drizzling

1 recipe Brick Oven–Style Dough (page 34)

All-purpose flour for rolling and dusting

¼ cup cornmeal for sprinkling

½ cup San Marzano Pizza Sauce (page 177)

8 ounces burrata cheese

Freshly ground black pepper

In a bowl, gently toss the squash blossoms with 1 tablespoon of olive oil.

Preheat the grill and the pizza oven insert on high heat, until the temperature reaches 650° to 700°F.

Divide the dough into 2 portions. Hand toss, or, on a floured surface, pat or roll each portion into a 12-inch-diameter circle.

Sprinkle a pizza peel or a flexible cutting board with half of the cornmeal. Arrange a pizza circle on the corn-meal-dusted peel. Brush with olive oil. Spread with half of the pizza sauce, leaving a ½-inch border. Slice the burrata into 8 slices and arrange 4 of the slices on top of the pizza. Then arrange half of the squash blossoms on top. Drizzle a little olive oil over each burrata slice and sprinkle with pepper.

Hold the pizza peel level with the grill rack so that the pizza will slide onto the center of the hot pizza stone. With a quick forward jerk of your arm, slide the pizza from the peel to the stone. Grill for 2 to 3 minutes, or until the cheese has melted slightly and the squash blossoms have browned on the edges. Slide the peel under the pizza and remove it from the pizza oven. Repeat the process with the other pizza.

**W**E SHARED A PIZZA TOPPED WITH PEA SHOOTS, NETTLES, RICOTTA, LEEKS, and lemon at Flour + Water in San Francisco and were inspired yet again! A little grated lemon zest on the ricotta makes a bold statement. There's a reason why nettles are also called *stinging nettles*. They grow wild in California and will sting your hands if you're not wearing gloves when you pick them. However, the sting goes away when the nettles are cooked. Just be careful when you work with them.

# PIZZA BIANCOVERDE

**MAKES 2
(12-INCH) PIZZAS**

1 cup nettles or thinly
sliced Belgian endive

2 tablespoons extra-virgin
olive oil, plus more for
brushing and drizzling

1 recipe Brick Oven–Style
Dough (page 34)

All-purpose flour
for rolling and dusting

¼ cup cornmeal
for sprinkling

½ cup thinly sliced leeks

½ cup pea shoots or
watercress

8 ounces ricotta cheese

Zest of 1 lemon

Preheat the grill and the pizza oven insert on high heat until the temperature reaches 650° to 700°F.

In a bowl and using tongs, gently toss the nettles with the 2 tablespoons of olive oil.

Divide the dough into 2 portions. Hand toss, or, on a floured surface, pat or roll each portion into a 12-inch-diameter circle.

Sprinkle a pizza peel or a flexible cutting board with half of the cornmeal. Arrange a pizza circle on the cornmeal-dusted peel. Brush with olive oil. Spread with half of the nettles and leeks, leaving a ½-inch border. Then, arrange half of the pea shoots on top, and dollop half of the ricotta cheese in various places. Sprinkle the ricotta dollops with lemon zest.

Hold the pizza peel level with the grill rack so that the pizza will slide onto the center of the hot pizza stone. With a quick forward jerk of your arm, slide the pizza from the peel to the stone. Grill for 2 to 3 minutes, or until the ricotta has melted and the nettles have browned on the edges. Slide the peel under the pizza and remove it from the pizza oven. Repeat the process with the other pizza.

TURNIP PIZZA? ARE WE KIDDING? NO. WHEN YOU FIGHT OVER WHO GETS to eat the turnips, you know this is good. When we were doing initial testing for this book at Smoke 'n' Fire in Overland Park, Kansas, we just sort of cleaned out the vegetable drawer to experiment with the pizza oven insert. We tried a pizza with thinly sliced turnips, turnip and mustard greens, and a little ham, and voilà!

# HAM, TURNIPS, ᴬᴺᴰ GREENS PIZZA

MAKES 2
(12-INCH) PIZZAS

4 medium-size turnips, peeled and thinly sliced

2 cups finely chopped turnip greens or stemmed and finely chopped mustard or collard greens

2 tablespoons extra-virgin olive oil, plus more for brushing and drizzling

1 recipe Brick Oven–Style Dough (page 34)

All-purpose flour for rolling and dusting

¼ cup cornmeal for sprinkling

1 cup finely chopped smoked ham

¼ cup finely grated Pecorino Romano cheese

Preheat the grill and the pizza oven insert on high heat until the temperature reaches 650° to 700°F.

In a bowl, gently toss the turnip slices and greens with 2 tablespoons of olive oil.

Divide the dough into 2 portions. Hand toss, or, on a floured surface, pat or roll each portion into a 12-inch-diameter circle.

Sprinkle a pizza peel or a flexible cutting board with half of the cornmeal. Arrange a pizza circle on the corn-meal-dusted peel. Brush with olive oil. Spread with half of the vegetables and ham, leaving a ½-inch border. Then, sprinkle with half of the cheese.

Hold the pizza peel level with the grill rack so that the pizza will slide onto the center of the hot pizza stone. With a quick forward jerk of your arm, slide the pizza from the peel to the stone. Grill for 2 to 3 minutes, or until the cheese has melted. Slide the peel under the pizza and remove it from the pizza oven. Repeat the process with the other pizza.

**K**AREN'S FRIEND MAUREEN HASSELTINE CREATED A BRILLIANT SIDE DISH of Roma tomatoes drizzled with extra-virgin olive oil and placed in a hot oven for 20 minutes. Then she quickly removed the pan and stuffed bunches of fresh basil leaves around the tomatoes, drizzled it with more olive oil, and returned to the hot oven for about 5 more minutes to "frizzle" the basil. Here is our version as a pizza with the tomato suggestions of Sun Gold (our favorite yellow cherry tomato) and Super Sweet 100 (our favorite red cherry tomato). The high heat turns these sweet tomatoes into even sweeter tomato bombs that pop with flavor.

# CHERRY TOMATO
# AND FRIZZLED HERB PIZZA

MAKES 2
(12-INCH) PIZZAS

**2 pints cherry tomatoes (use Sun Gold and Super Sweet 100, if available)**

**1 recipe Brick Oven–Style Dough (page 34)**

**All-purpose flour for rolling and dusting**

**¼ cup cornmeal for sprinkling**

**Extra-virgin olive oil for brushing and drizzling**

**1 cup packed fresh basil leaves**

**Kosher or sea salt**

Preheat the grill and the pizza oven insert on high heat until the temperature reaches 650° to 700°F.

Slice two-thirds of the red and yellow cherry tomatoes in half and leave one-third of the smallest tomatoes whole.

Divide the dough into 2 portions. Hand toss, or, on a floured surface, pat or roll each portion into a 12-inch-diameter circle.

Sprinkle a pizza peel or a flexible cutting board with half of the cornmeal. Arrange a pizza circle on the corn-meal-dusted peel. Brush with olive oil. Spread with half of the tomatoes, leaving a ½-inch border. Tuck half of the basil leaves evenly among the tomatoes, drizzle with extra-virgin olive oil and sprinkle with salt.

Hold the pizza peel level with the grill rack so that the pizza will slide onto the center of the hot pizza stone. With a quick forward jerk of your arm, slide the pizza from the

*(recipe continues)*

peel to the stone. Grill for 2 to 3 minutes, or until the basil leaves have frizzled. Slide the peel under the pizza and remove it from the pizza oven. Repeat the process with the other pizza.

Salad on the Side

# PANZANELLA

**SERVES 6** (*but 4 people will devour it*)

An Italian-style pizzeria book wouldn't be complete without panzanella, a classic Tuscan bread salad. This begs to be made in the summer when cucumbers and tomatoes come fresh off the vine and basil is prolific. According to Gina Stipo, a culinary teacher and cookbook author who lives in Tuscany, the bread is best if you buy it two or three days in advance and let it sit on the counter, uncovered, to get stale and hard.

½ loaf stale rustic artisan bread (see headnote)

2 or 3 large ripe tomatoes, diced

1 red onion, diced

1 cucumber, diced

¼ cup chopped fresh basil

1 tablespoon red wine vinegar

½ cup extra-virgin olive oil, preferably Tuscan

Sea salt and freshly ground black pepper

Cube the stale bread and place in a large bowl. Add the tomatoes, onion, cucumber, basil, vinegar, and olive oil and toss to coat well. Adjust the seasoning to taste. Add more olive oil, if needed. Let sit at room temperature for at least 30 minutes so the bread soaks up all the good juices and softens somewhat.

**TIP:** *Tuscan olive oil (another tip from Gina Stipo) is available in fine gourmet shops and is also available at Costco under its Kirkland label. It has a unique peppery finish and is perfect for drizzling over this salad, bruschetta, panini, and pizzas.*

**T**HE TRICK TO THIS PIZZA IS FINISHING IT WITH SOME FRESH SLICES OF fig and tearing the mozzarella instead of slicing it. It gives it a nice three-dimensional rustic finish.

# FIG AND PROSCIUTTO PIZZA

**MAKES 2 (12-INCH) PIZZAS**

8 figs

1 recipe Brick Oven–Style Dough (page 34)

All-purpose flour for rolling and dusting

¼ cup cornmeal for sprinkling

Extra-virgin olive oil for brushing and drizzling

12 paper-thin slices prosciutto

8 ounces buffalo mozzarella cheese

Preheat the grill and the pizza oven insert on high heat until the temperature reaches 650° to 700°F.

Slice half of the figs and set aside for the final topping. Quarter the remaining figs.

Divide the dough into 2 portions. Hand toss, or, on a floured surface, pat or roll each portion into a 12-inch-diameter circle.

Sprinkle a pizza peel or a flexible cutting board with half of the cornmeal. Arrange a pizza circle on the corn-meal-dusted peel. Brush with olive oil. Arrange 6 slices of prosciutto on the dough, then 8 fig quarters, and then half of the mozzarella, torn into small pieces.

Hold the pizza peel level with the grill rack so that the pizza will slide onto the center of the hot pizza stone. With a quick forward jerk of your arm, slide the pizza from the peel to the stone. Grill for 2 to 3 minutes, or until the cheese has melted. Slide the peel under the pizza and remove it from the pizza oven. Arrange half of the slices of fig on the pizza and drizzle with additional olive oil. Repeat the process with the other pizza.

**P**IZZA BELLA IN KANSAS CITY BOASTS A WOOD-FIRED OVEN AND NO OTHER cooking appliances in the restaurant. Their pizzas are delicious, but the oven-roasted Brussels sprouts are divine. We couldn't resist making them part of the pizza.

# SHAVED BRUSSELS SPROUT PIZZA WITH RED ONION, PECORINO, AND PANCETTA

MAKES 2 (12-INCH) PIZZAS

1 recipe Brick Oven–Style Dough (page 34)

All-purpose flour for rolling and dusting

¼ cup cornmeal for sprinkling

Extra-virgin olive oil for brushing and drizzling

1 pound Brussels sprouts, trimmed and shredded in a food processor

1 cup diced pancetta, cooked until crisp

8 ounces buffalo mozzarella cheese, shredded

1 cup grated Pecorino cheese

1 red onion, thinly sliced into rings

Preheat the grill and the pizza oven insert on high heat until the temperature reaches 650° to 700°F.

Divide the dough into 2 portions. Hand toss, or, on a floured surface, pat or roll each portion into a 12-inch-diameter circle.

Sprinkle a pizza peel or a flexible cutting board with half of the cornmeal. Arrange a pizza circle on the cornmeal-dusted peel. Brush with olive oil. Arrange half of the shredded Brussels sprouts and pancetta on the dough. Top with half of the cheeses and half of the onion rings.

Hold the pizza peel level with the grill rack so that the pizza will slide onto the center of the hot pizza stone. With a quick forward jerk of your arm, slide the pizza from the peel to the stone. Grill for 2 to 3 minutes, or until the mozzarella has melted and the sprouts have browned on the edges. Slide the peel under the pizza and remove it from the pizza oven. Repeat the process with the other pizza.

GINA STIPO OF ECCO LA CUCINA IN SIENA INTRODUCED US TO PANUOZZI, from the Campania region of Italy. She says, "They're a sandwich from the pizza oven. Ciabatta-shaped loaves of dough are flash-baked in the pizza oven, and then sliced open and layered with cheese and meats or vegetables. They go back into the hot pizza oven open-faced for a couple minutes to melt the cheese. Close them and cut them in two or three large slices. Delish!" We've re-created her favorite of salami, mozzarella, and broccoli rabe.

# PANUOZZO SALSICCIA

SERVES 2 OR 3

1 recipe Classic Pizza Dough (page 33)

All-purpose flour for rolling and dusting

2 tablespoons extra-virgin olive oil, plus more for brushing and drizzling

2 cups chopped broccoli rabe

2 tablespoons cornmeal for sprinkling

6 paper-thin slices salami

6 slices buffalo mozzarella cheese

Preheat the grill and the pizza oven insert on high heat until the temperature reaches 650° to 700°F.

On a floured surface, form the dough into a long, flat loaf, about 1 inch high, 6 inches wide, and 9 inches long.

In a sauté pan over medium heat on the stovetop, heat 2 tablespoons olive oil and cook the broccoli rabe for 7 to 8 minutes, until tender.

Sprinkle a pizza peel or a flexible cutting board with the cornmeal. Place the dough on the cornmeal-dusted peel. Brush with olive oil.

Hold the pizza peel level with the grill rack so that the loaf of bread will slide onto the center of the hot pizza stone. With a quick forward jerk of your arm, slide the dough from the peel to the stone. Grill for 2 to 3 minutes, or until the dough has risen and browned. Slide the peel under the bread and remove it from the pizza oven. An instant-read thermometer inserted into the middle of the loaf should register 190°F.

Using a kitchen towel to protect your hands, cut the bread horizontally with a bread or serrated knife. Brush the insides lightly with olive oil and spread the chopped broccoli rabe to the edges of the bread. Layer the salami and mozzarella evenly over the broccoli rabe. Place the open-face sandwich and the top slice of bread both back on the peel and slide back into the oven for about 1 minute to warm through and melt the cheese. Remove from the oven and place the top on the sandwich. Cut into 2 or 3 slices and eat while warm.

**P**ANUOZZI ARE BIG SANDWICHES MADE FROM PIZZA DOUGH THAT ARE shaped like a long, flat loaf of bread and baked in a wood-fired pizza oven. After they bake, they are sliced lengthwise while hot, layered with fillings, and popped back in the pizza oven to melt the cheese and warm the other ingredients. They are great take-away food or street food because they are easy to hold and especially because they are quick to prepare. Here is a classic mix of dry-cured pancetta, provolone, black pepper, and artichokes.

# PANUOZZO
# ALLA PANCETTA

SERVES 2 OR 3

1 recipe Classic Pizza Dough (page 33)

All-purpose flour for rolling and dusting

2 tablespoons cornmeal for sprinkling

Extra-virgin olive oil for brushing and drizzling

1½ cups chopped artichoke hearts (jarred or canned)

6 paper-thin slices dry-cured pancetta

6 slices provolone cheese

Freshly ground black pepper

Preheat the grill and the pizza oven insert on high heat until the temperature reaches 650° to 700°F.

On a floured surface, form the dough into a long, flat loaf, about 1 inch high, 6 inches wide, and 9 inches long.

Sprinkle a pizza peel or a flexible cutting board with the cornmeal. Place the dough on the cornmeal-dusted peel. Brush with olive oil.

Hold the pizza peel level with the grill rack so that the dough will slide onto the center of the hot pizza stone. With a quick forward jerk of your arm, slide the dough from the peel to the stone. Grill for 2 to 3 minutes, or until the dough has risen and browned. Slide the peel under the bread and remove it from the pizza oven. An instant-read thermometer inserted into the middle of the loaf should register 190°F.

Using a kitchen towel to protect your hands, cut the bread horizontally with a bread or serrated knife. Brush the insides lightly with olive oil and spread the artichokes to the edges of the bottom piece of bread. Layer the pancetta and provolone evenly over the artichokes. Sprinkle with freshly ground black pepper. Place the bottom and top of the bread both back on the peel and slide back into the oven for about 1 minute to warm through and melt the cheese. Remove from the oven and place the top on the sandwich. Cut into 2 or 3 slices and eat while warm.

WE LIKE THE MIX AND MATCH OF ITALIAN AND FRENCH INGREDIENTS in this pizza. The garlic cream sauce is a classic French white sauce with the addition of garlic. The porcini mushrooms and pancetta are Italian, while the Gruyere de Comte is a creamier Gruyère from France. Then we let you decide whether you want to top it off with Italian arugula or French frisée, *bien sûr*.

# FRENCH–ITALIAN BORDER PIZZA

MAKES 2
(12-INCH) PIZZAS

**For the garlic cream sauce:**

3 tablespoons unsalted butter

2 garlic cloves, minced

3 tablespoons all-purpose flour

1½ cups milk

½ teaspoon sea salt

¼ teaspoon freshly ground white pepper

**For the pizzas:**

2 tablespoons unsalted butter

1 pound yellow onions, chopped

6 ounces pancetta, diced

1 pound porcini mushrooms, brushed off with a dry cloth and chopped

2 tablespoons extra-virgin olive oil, plus more for brushing and drizzling

1 recipe Brick Oven–Style Dough (page 34)

All-purpose flour for rolling and dusting

¼ cup cornmeal for sprinkling

6 ounces Comte (Gruyère) cheese, shredded

¾ cup loosely packed arugula or frisée

Kosher or sea salt and freshly ground black pepper

For the garlic cream sauce, over medium heat on the stovetop, melt the 3 tablespoons of butter in a saucepan and add the garlic, stirring for about 1 minute, until lightly browned. Add the flour and stir for another minute to incorporate and make a paste (called a roux). Add the milk ½ cup at a time and whisk to blend while it thickens. Add the sea salt and the white pepper and stir to blend. The sauce should be smooth. Cover and set aside.

Preheat the grill and the pizza oven insert on high heat until the temperature reaches 650° to 700°F.

For the pizzas, over medium-high heat in a sauté pan on the stovetop, melt the 2 tablespoons of butter and add the onions and pancetta. Cook for 3 or 4 minutes, until the onions are soft and the pancetta begins to brown. Add the mushrooms, drizzle with the 2 tablespoons of olive oil, and toss to coat. Cook for 3 or 4 more minutes.

Divide the dough into 2 portions. Hand toss, or, on a floured surface, pat or roll each portion into a 12-inch-diameter circle.

Sprinkle a pizza peel or a flexible cutting board with half of the cornmeal. Arrange a pizza circle on the cornmeal-dusted peel. Spread half of the garlic cream sauce to the rim of each pizza, then spoon half of the onion mixture evenly over the sauce. Top with half of the cheese.

Hold the pizza peel level with the grill rack so that the pizza will slide onto the center of the hot pizza stone. With a quick forward jerk of your arm, slide the pizza from the peel to the stone. Grill for 2 to 3 minutes, or until the cheese has melted. Slide the peel under the pizza and remove it from the pizza oven. Top with a frill of half of the arugula and adjust the seasoning to taste. Repeat the process with the other pizza.

**G**ORGONZOLA MAKES THIS A BLUE CHEESE LOVER'S FANTASY PIZZA. THE dolce means "sweet." This blue cheese is milder, softer, and melts faster than regular Gorgonzola, but regular will do just fine.

# GORGONZOLA DOLCE PIZZA
## WITH FINGERLINGS AND RADICCHIO

MAKES 2
(12-INCH) PIZZAS

1 recipe Brick Oven–Style Dough (page 34)

All-purpose flour for rolling and dusting

¼ cup cornmeal for sprinkling

2 tablespoons extra-virgin olive oil, plus more for brushing and drizzling

1 pound fingerling potatoes, cut in half lengthwise

Kosher or sea salt and freshly ground black pepper

2 cups shredded radicchio

8 ounces Gorgonzola dolce cheese, crumbled

2 teaspoons chopped fresh rosemary

Preheat the grill and the pizza oven insert on high heat until the temperature reaches 650° to 700°F.

In a sauté pan on the stovetop, heat 2 tablespoons olive oil over medium-high heat. Parcook the fingerlings for 8 to 10 minutes, or until just fork-tender.

Divide the dough into 2 portions. Hand toss, or, on a floured surface, pat or roll each portion into a 12-inch-diameter circle.

Sprinkle a pizza peel or a flexible cutting board with half of the cornmeal. Arrange a pizza circle on the corn-meal-dusted peel. Brush with olive oil. Arrange half of the potatoes and season to taste. Then add half of the radicchio and half of the Gorgonzola on the dough. Sprinkle with half of the rosemary and drizzle with olive oil.

Hold the pizza peel level with the grill rack so that the pizza will slide onto the center of the hot pizza stone. With a quick forward jerk of your arm, slide the pizza from the peel to the stone. Grill for 2 to 3 minutes, or until the Gorgonzola has melted and the radicchio has browned on the edges. Slide the peel under the pizza and remove it from the pizza oven. Repeat the process with the other pizza.

# INDEX

Note: Page references in *italics* indicate recipe photographs.